Copyright Clarity

Copyright
Clarity

How Fair Use
Supports Digital Learning

RENEE HOBBS

Foreword by Donna Alvermann

A JOINT PUBLICATION

CORWIN
A SAGE Company

NCTE National Council of
Teachers of English

For information:

Corwin
A SAGE Company
2455 Teller Road
Thousand Oaks, California 91320
(800) 233-9936
Fax: (800) 417-2466
www.corwinpress.com

SAGE Pvt. Ltd.
B 1/I 1 Mohan Cooperative
   Industrial Area
Mathura Road, New Delhi 110 044
India

SAGE Ltd.
1 Oliver's Yard
55 City Road
London EC1Y 1SP
United Kingdom

SAGE Asia-Pacific Pte. Ltd.
33 Pekin Street #02-01
Far East Square
Singapore 048763

Printed in the United States of America

Library of Congress Cataloging-in-Publication Data

Hobbs, Renee.
Copyright clarity: how fair use supports digital learning/Renee Hobbs; foreword by Donna Alvermann.
         p. cm.
"A Joint Publication With the National Council of Teachers of English."
Includes bibliographical references and index.
ISBN 978-1-4129-8159-0 (pbk. : alk. paper)
    1. Distance education—Computer-assisted instruction—United States.
2. Copyright and distance education—United States. 3. Internet in education—Law and legislation—United States. 4. Digital media—Law and legislation—United States. 5. Mass media and education—United States. 6. Fair use (Copyright)—United States. I. National Council of Teachers of English. II. Title.

LC5803.C65H63 2010
371.3'58—dc22

This book is printed on acid-free paper.

10 11 12 13 14   10 9 8 7 6 5 4 3 2 1

Acquisitions Editor:	Carol Chambers Collins
Editorial Assistant:	Allison Scott
Production Editor:	Veronica Stapleton
Copy Editor:	Adam Dunham
Typesetter:	C&M Digitals (P) Ltd.
Proofreader:	Jennifer Gritt
Indexer:	Sheila Bodell
Cover Designer:	Michael Dubowe
Illustrator:	Priscilla Bell

Contents

Foreword

*C*opyright Clarity: How Fair Use Supports Digital Learning is a book that will make a significant difference in how I design my college courses for K–12 classroom teachers, media specialists, and school librarians from this point forward. In fact, I cannot imagine writing another syllabus without Renee Hobbs's book close at hand. It is that essential.

For too long a time, copyright "law" had eluded me, and like many other colleagues who were equally unsure about their rights and responsibilities as users, I simply avoided numerous forms of copyrighted materials that undoubtedly would have enhanced both my instruction and my students' learning. Although I was vaguely aware of the doctrine of fair use, I had assumed wrongly that, in principle, it was a concept meant to work against me. I now know differently, thanks to Renee Hobbs, who has written an immensely readable text on why fair use is actually an ally of teachers and students immersed in 21st-century literacies.

All of this was brought home to me when a student in one of my methods classes this semester used the term "copyfright" to signal her concern that a project she was planning on fan fiction for a high school English class might be in violation of certain copyright guidelines as she understood them. I realized then that *Copyright Clarity* could not go to press soon enough. I wanted to give this student a copy of the book, but since that was impossible, we talked through some of the issues Hobbs lays out in a chapter that explains a process K–12 educators and teacher educators can employ to determine the rights and responsibilities of fair use. Going through that process provided the self-confidence I needed to address questions from other students who had similar concerns about using copyrighted materials for their final projects.

Copyright Clarity is more than a simple eye opener on fair use, however. It deftly teaches, as well. Real-world examples abound, and there are several opportunities for the reader to engage in an inquiry process while turning the pages. In fact, I found myself dog earring numerous pages as I read, promising myself that no longer would I let certain assumptions (even myths) about seeking permissions deter me from incorporating copyrighted materials that I needed to make learning both meaningful and memorable in my students' eyes.

Finally, a book on topics as sensitive as copyright and fair use must provide documentation that is above reproach. Here, Renee Hobbs' scholarship and experience as a media literacy educator instilled the credibility that I was seeking. In a nutshell, *Copyright Clarity* is easily the most important book I have read this year.

Donna E. Alvermann
University of Georgia

Preface

Perhaps you're wondering why you should even pick up this book. What do educators really need to know about copyright?

Well, it turns out that we're in the middle of a great civic and cultural awakening about the topic of copyright and fair use, one that's increasing in visibility and importance as a result of the Internet and communications technology. Educators have a vital role to play in this process.

The doctrine of fair use is central to the enterprise of education— and this book shows why educational leaders and classroom teachers must join scholars, librarians, and others to understand their responsibilities and to advocate for their rights under copyright law.

I was motivated to write this book when I found myself sitting in the audience at a major educational technology conference, in a room filled with 150 people, listening to a presenter who was scaring teachers to death with distorted and inaccurate misinformation about copyright. People left the room more unsure and more fearful than when they arrived. This book provides a genuine alternative to the doom-and-gloom message you might be familiar with, the one that tells you, "Just *don't* do it."

I promise: This book will forever change the way you think about copyright.

After reading this book, you'll have a confident understanding in the role that copyright and fair use play in promoting the development of students' literacy and learning. You and your students will be able to be truly *responsible* in using copyrighted materials and be able to take advantage of your *rights* under the doctrine of fair use. Most importantly, you'll have the knowledge you need to share these ideas with friends, family, colleagues, and others who care about the future of 21st-century literacy and learning.

Acknowledgments

Like many teachers, my computer laptop and office files are full of copyrighted materials: newspaper articles, book chapters, lesson plans, photos, films and videos, and computer programs. I'm lucky to have learned a lot about copyright and fair use over the years. But there won't be any legal jargon in this book because I'm not a legal expert, and this isn't the kind of book you can use to get free legal advice.

Before I began this project, I was pretty confused about copyright myself. I thought that only lawyers had the right to answer copyright questions. That's one of the myths of copyright that needs to be corrected. It seems that, when it comes to copyright, there's so much anxiety and insecurity about the topic that everyone—even lawyers—adopt a deferential tone, hypercautious in their interpretation of the law.

However, it turns out that, according to the law itself, *citizens themselves must interpret and apply the doctrine of fair use according to the specifics of each context and situation.*

How do educators gain the confidence to do this? Inspiring leadership has come from people like Carrie Russell at the Office for Information Technology Policy of the American Library Association (ALA), who has worked to make copyright law accessible to librarians and citizens nationwide. She reminds us that people must make a fair use determination based on sound judgment and the careful consideration of the situation at hand. She writes, "Those who prefer a 'yes' or 'no' answer may be troubled by the ambiguous nature of fair use, but fair use cannot be reduced to a checklist. Fair use requires that people *think*."[1] This book is motivated by the desire to promote the kind of critical thinking that Carrie Russell recognizes as essential for both teachers and learners alike.

I'm particularly grateful to Patricia Aufderheide of the Center for Social Media at American University, who launched me on this journey by sharing her passion, helping me to understand that copyright and fair use is a free-speech issue. Pat's approach to scholarship-in-action is a model of inspiration to me. When Pat introduced me to Peter Jaszi, a distinguished legal scholar at American University Washington College of Law, I was in for a treat. Day by day, my understanding of copyright grew until I felt confident enough to share my knowledge with students and colleagues.

Pat, Peter, and I were truly honored to receive financial support from the John D. and Catherine T. MacArthur Foundation to create *The Code of Best Practices in Media Literacy Education*. My research assistant, Katie Donnelly, provided valued support for this project. Kristin Hokanson, David Cooper Moore, and Michael RobbGrieco all developed creative resources that helped this project to thrive. Thanks also go to the more than 200 educators from across the nation who helped us clarify how copyright applies to their work in a series of interviews and focus-group meetings. Kenneth Crews of Columbia University provided valuable insight on this project by sharing his expertise on copyright in education. Most of all, I would like to thank Professor Peter Jaszi, on whose brilliance, kindness, and expertise I have relied. The most important concepts presented in this book are those I have learned from him.

Corwin wishes to acknowledge the following peer reviewers for their editorial insight and guidance.

Gerard A. Dery, Principal
Nessacus Regional Middle School
Dalton, Massachusetts

Inez Liftig, Eighth Grade Science Teacher
Fairfield Woods Middle School
Fairfield, Connecticut

Cheryl Steele Oakes, Collaborative Content Coach for Technology
Wells Ogunquit Community School District
Wells, Maine

Jason Thompson, Assistant Principal
Schalmont Central School District
Schenectady, New York

Mary Tipton, Director, Technology and Distance Education
Kent State University
Kent, Ohio

About the Author

 Renee Hobbs is one of the nation's leading authorities on media literacy education. She spearheaded the development of the *Journal of Media Literacy Education* to support the work of media literacy educators and scholars. She has created numerous award-winning videos, Web sites, and multimedia curriculum materials for K–12 educators and offers professional development programs to educators in school districts across the United States. Her research examines the impact of media literacy education on academic achievement and has been published in more than 50 scholarly and professional books and journals. She is a professor at the School of Communications and Theater at Temple University in Philadelphia and holds a joint appointment at the College of Education. She received an EdD from the Harvard Graduate School of Education, an MA in communication from the University of Michigan, and a BA with a double major in English literature and film video studies from the University of Michigan.

In the 21st century, teachers and students are using mass media, popular culture, and digital technologies to support the learning process.

1

Copyright Matters for 21st-Century Learning

I began teaching teachers about media literacy back in the 1980s, when VHS tapes were the latest technology—it was the age of dinosaurs, it now seems. I would bring in a handful of tapes, which I had cued up, including excerpts from TV news, advertising, movies and popular television programming to demonstrate a variety of instructional techniques for developing critical analysis skills in responding to mass media and popular culture and show how creative media production activities support literacy and learning in English language arts, social studies, and health education.[1] Today, because media literacy is mandated in nearly all of the state curriculum frameworks, I cross the country offering teacher workshops. To develop learning activities for media literacy, I now use my digital video recorder to record television programs, manipulating and storing clips on my laptop.

Today, educators are discovering that 21st-century learners benefit from approaches that build creativity, critical thinking, and problem solving skills in the context of civic literacy and global awareness.[2] Students now make active use of multimedia texts, tools, and technologies. They are engaged in collaborative, hands-on work as both readers and writers of messages in print, visual, electronic, and digital forms.

But with every group of teachers I work with, there's a question that always comes up with an increasing spirit of trepidation: "Is it legal to use copyrighted material like this?"

"Of course," I say. Like many media literacy educators, I use copyrighted materials under the doctrine of fair use, Section 107 of the Copyright Law of 1976. Users have the right to use copyrighted materials without payment or permission, depending on the specific context and situation of the use.

It is ironic that, at a time when online digital technologies are enabling educators to create and share an ever-widening array of texts, sounds, still and moving images, music, and graphic art, we are seeing a dramatic increase in the climate of fear among educators concerning the use of these resources for teaching and learning. And since fear reduces innovation, those of us who promote the use of digital media as tools for teaching and learning need to sit up and take notice.

Educators and Students Use Copyrighted Materials

With the rise of the Internet, it is becoming easier and easier to find and use documents, primary sources, and other materials including articles, documents, images, videos, games, and music. Nearly everything online is copyrighted.

And even the simple act of reading may trigger copyright issues. For example, when you read something online, you must make a digital copy of it to access it. So, copying is deeply implicated in the very act of using a computer.

Children and young people have a vast array of choices for information and entertainment. In this mediated childhood, they are simultaneously consuming and creating large quantities of media messages.[3] According to a recent encyclopedia on children, adolescents, and the media,[4] here's some of what's happening.

- Parents buy Baby Einstein videos for their infants in the mistaken belief that they build cognitive or perceptual skills.
- Preschoolers are watching the Sprout cable channel, a 24-hour channel just for them. They are lap-surfing with their moms, and practicing their social networking skills playing Club Penguin when they are six.
- By the time children are eight years old, they will generally be spending eight hours daily in some form of media-consumption experience, whether that be watching television or movies, playing videogames, sharing text messages, or listening to music.

- Children enjoy online games and post to social networking Web sites or talk with friends online.
- By high school, some teens are uploading photos, writing snappy captions, and putting their own poetry, art, and writing online.
- Student-produced videos, created over the weekend by friends just for fun—or for an assignment in Latin, biology, or history—are uploaded to YouTube, where they can be seen by millions.

As a result, parents, educators, and civic leaders are all beginning to recognize the need for a new set of competencies that are essential for engagement and cultural participation in 21st-century society. These include the four components of the definition of *media literacy,* which was developed at a convening at the Aspen Institute in 1993: "the ability to access, analyze, evaluate and communicate messages in a wide variety of forms."[5] As British media scholar Sonia Livingstone has explained,

> Each component supports the others as part of a nonlinear, dynamic learning process. Learning to create content helps one to analyze that produced professionally by others; skills in analysis and evaluation open the doors to new uses of the Internet, expanding access, and so forth.[6]

Media literacy learning occurs at the college and university level, in high schools and elementary schools, with parents, and in environments like adult education, youth media, and public-access centers. Media literacy education vitally depends on the ability of educators to be able to use and manipulate copyrighted materials from digital media, mass media, and popular culture.

While they come from many different disciplines and types of educational backgrounds, educators who make use of media literacy concepts share a focus on critical inquiry.[7] They often use the instructional method of close analysis or deconstruction, as well as formal and informal media production activities. Viewing and discussion activities are also common.

But today's media literacy teachers operate in an environment where practically every object of interest is protected by copyright. Typically, they teach analytic skills with examples of photojournalism, news, documentary, advertising, reality shows, comedies, sports programs, music videos, videogames, Web sites, and even home-shopping shows. A growing number of educators make active educational use of downloaded videos from user-generated content sites such as YouTube. Some access music or spoken-word files from purchases at iTunes or Audible. They often teach production skills along with critical thinking by encouraging students to produce new work that in part comments on or draws from existing work, capitalizing on students' appetite for popular-culture consumption and creative activities.

Here are some teachers who make use of media literacy educational practices:

Sarah Wing, a second-grade teacher at the Russell Byers Charter School in Philadelphia, explores the topic of media violence with her students. She invites students to talk about movies they have seen that might have scared them. They discuss the difference between realistic violence and fantasy violence and learn about using the film ratings to make decisions about what kinds of shows are appropriate and inappropriate for them.

Heidi Whitus, a teacher at the Communication Arts High School in San Antonio, Texas, videotapes off-air from television shows using a VCR. Heidi digitizes parts of the television programs and movies that she wants to use in the classroom and converts them to QuickTime files so she can use them in the classroom or reproduce them so her students can use them. She uses these clips to discuss and analyze the form and structure of visual media, exploring how issues of authorship, representation, technology, and culture are expressed in each work.

Cyndy Scheibe, a psychology professor and director of Project Look Sharp, a media literacy initiative at Ithaca College, uses comic strips from newspapers to involve students in a critique and commentary of the values messages have embedded in them. Her team at Project Look Sharp has created online curriculum materials about the media's representation of the Middle East that features clips from the Disney film, *Aladdin.* Another curriculum on the representation of war makes use of *Newsweek* magazine covers depicting the Vietnam War, the Gulf War, and the conflict in Afghanistan.

Caleb Smith, who teaches film and video at the Capital Area School for the Arts in Harrisburg, Pennsylvania, uses a "falsification" assignment, where he gives students dubbed and digitized copies of television programs and teaches editing by asking students to reedit a particular scene differently to communicate a different meaning than the original episode. In viewing the completed projects, students discover that meaning can be created through juxtaposition and sequencing.

Kristin Hokanson, a technology integration specialist at Upper Merion High School, helps teachers use digital media for teaching and learning. In one situation, she helped the biology teacher develop an assignment where students created a "virtual zoo," developing Web pages to share their knowledge about specific animal species.

Why Do Educators Care About Copyright and Fair Use?

Educators have a set of shared beliefs and attitudes regarding the use of intellectual property as a tool for teaching and learning.[8] We believe:

Cultural criticism is essential to democracy. Educators value cultural criticism as an essential tool for self-actualization and democracy. "A literate citizenship cannot be created if the people who control images don't allow them to be used," Cyndy Scheibe explained in an interview. "It's important that users of media participate in it and don't just receive it."[9] In contemporary culture, students are trained to be consumers of media—that is why it's important to go beyond this role to become authors and creators themselves.

Mass and digital media are an important part of the cultural environment. Teachers know that mass media and popular culture are part of the cultural landscape, deeply connected to students' sense of personal and social identity. "Copyrighted materials are like our cultural landscape—you need to be able to use and analyze media,"[10] said one teacher whom we interviewed. Sharing our interpretations and understandings of the diverse works of expression and communication around us is an important part of learning to make sense of the world. Media are a part of our lives in a way that it wasn't 20 or 30 years, ago, said media educator and video artist Diane Nerwen: "We should have access to our culture and be able to talk about it and comment on the world around us. If we don't comment on it, then it feels like information is being controlled."[11]

The effective use of copyrighted materials enhances the teaching and learning process. A college professor who teaches preservice teachers talked about the importance of using copyrighted works in educational settings because they provide more current examples than offered in most textbooks. Contemporary mass media materials hook attention and interest, and they help teachers connect new ideas to students' existing base of knowledge. "Teaching is just better when we can pull from a lot of different sources," said Frank Baker, a media literacy advocate and teacher educator in Columbia, South Carolina. "Imitation is a way to learn," he explained in an interview. "If students can't take and use the most highly developed messages that society creates, it's a handicap for them and the whole society."[12]

Appropriation of cultural materials promotes creativity and learning. There is significant educational value to the process of juxtaposition and recombination of existing copyrighted materials. Young people are creating remixes and mashups, where existing copyrighted works are juxtaposed and recombined with original materials to create new works. Teachers are exploring this technique, too. For example, an art teacher asks students to select a famous painting of the 17th or 18th century and use image manipulation software to "put themselves into the image." The assignment connects learning about art to learning about technology as a way to promote reflection on personal and social identity. But there are limits to appropriation, as Faith Rogow, former president of the National Association for Media Literacy Education has pointed out. "It shouldn't be a free-for-all, but instead a thoughtful process"[13] in which students take material in which they can recontextualize, to make it their own. But appropriation is a powerful instructional tool for student learning. As Rogow explained, "Mashups are an opportunity for students to really look at the media they consume—to take it and give it their own spin. It helps show kids how they can present their own point of view."[14]

Copyright owners and users of copyrighted materials both deserve respect. Educators respect the rights of copyright owners and deeply value the creative work of authors. Many educators have themselves created curriculum materials; others have written articles, books, or created videos and multimedia products. Many educators see themselves as copyright owners as well as users. As a result, most media literacy educators articulate a strong sense of appreciation for the need to protect the rights of creative people through copyright. Media literacy educators share certain values about the use of copyrighted material, including news, advertising, movies, music, videogames, and other aspects of mass media, digital media, and popular culture. While they respect the rights of owners of intellectual property, they also believe that it is necessary to use copyrighted works freely for the purpose of strengthening students' critical thinking and communication skills.

From Copyright Confusion to Copyright Clarity

There's a lot of copyright confusion out there in the world of education. Some educators attempt studied ignorance, believing that increased knowledge about copyright would impede their work. Still others close the doors of the classroom and keep quiet about the use of copyrighted materials in order to avoid potential conflict.

The most troubling thing is that all this copyright confusion has a price: Teachers' lack of knowledge about copyright and fair use affects the quality of teaching and learning.

It limits the distribution of curriculum materials and resources, thus affecting students' overall media literacy learning. Plus, most teachers do not teach about the law of copyright and fair use because they themselves do not understand it. As a result, students do not learn that copyright is designed to protect both the rights of owners and users in order to promote creativity and innovation.

As we will see in Chapter 2, teachers aren't alone; actually, there is widespread confusion about copyright among most people in American society. Even information professionals are confused. Many people receive misinformation informally from their family, friends, colleagues, and supervisors. At some businesses and educational institutions, school policies are far more restrictive than the law mandates. Some people have tried to publish books, videos, or curriculum materials that include excerpts from copyrighted works, but found publishers unreceptive due to concerns about quoting from films, TV shows, advertising, popular culture, and online digital media.

For educators, one big problem is the widespread misunderstanding of the so-called "educational use guidelines," those negotiated agreements between media companies and some educational groups that present a list of hard-and-fast rules defining fair use. These guidelines are not the law. They do not define either the "safe harbors" or the "outer limits" of fair use. Relying on these guidelines actually hurts educators. Some legal scholars fear that if the educational community accepts these educational use guidelines in policy statements or in settling litigation, the concept of fair use will be weakened and narrowed, not strengthened. Columbia University legal scholar Kenneth Crews points out, when the community actually uses these guidelines and adheres to them, they reshape the normative understanding of the law, sacrificing the flexible nature of the concept of fair use.[15]

CITE YOUR SOURCES

Attribution (citing sources) is the practice of acknowledging the use of other people's ideas as part of your own work. Attribution is based on the principle of respecting the creative work of others. Attribution takes many forms. Journalists acknowledge "who said what" through statements like, "According to so-and-so, an expert in such-and-such. . . ." In scholarly and academic writing, there are many different forms of attribution that rely on citations using conventions established by professional associations like the Modern Language Association (MLA), the American Psychological Association (APA), and others. These conventions for citing sources relate to specific disciplines and fields. People have different expectations for how attribution works in books, newspaper articles, movies, and other genres. We don't expect much attribution in TV news, for example. In online media, the hyperlink can be used as form of attribution.

Plagiarism is using someone else's work without attribution. We think of plagiarism as "cut and paste" writing. Sometimes, plagiarism results from ignorance about the practice of attribution; other times, plagiarism can be accidental.

Although the conduct of plagiarism may overlap with copyright infringement, the two concepts are distinct. You can plagiarize from Shakespeare, but you'll never have a copyright problem, since his works are in the public domain. Plagiarism is an ethical problem handled by teachers and schools; copyright infringement is a legal problem handled by courts.

Transformativeness: It Will "Shake Your World"

Over 2,500 years ago, Aristotle explained that people create new ideas from old ideas. Since there are no new ideas under the sun, creativity consists of bringing old ideas together in new ways. As I write this book about copyright and fair use, for example, I am weaving together my ideas with the ideas and information I have learned from many other authors. You can see the sources I use by checking out the Endnotes provided in the back of the book.

Sharing ideas and information is part of the essential nature of all learning. Making reference to, using or quoting from the work of others is an example of fair use. I don't need to ask authors' permission or pay someone to quote from their work as I develop my own ideas. *Transformativeness* is the term emerging for the repurposing of copyrighted materials as part of the creative process. With the rise of digital media, transformativeness is becoming a valuable concept in both education and copyright law.

Joyce Valenza, a school library media specialist at Springfield High School in suburban Philadelphia, wrote about how liberating it was to learn about transformativeness in relation to the doctrine of fair use. She wrote a blog for *School Library Journal* explaining how a fresh understanding of fair use "shook her world," replacing a more conservative position on copyright that she had developed over the years, where she had discouraged students from *ever* using copyrighted materials in their own work.[16]

Most exciting to Valenza was that when her students created something new, using excerpts from copyrighted materials and claiming fair use, they can distribute the materials freely, on any kind of print, video, or online media platform. She wrote, "If a student has repurposed and added value to copyrighted material, she should be able to use it beyond the classroom (on YouTube, for instance) as well as within it."[17]

But, not everything that might be considered educationally beneficial is transformative. When teachers make multiple photocopies of a textbook, as a substitute for a purchase because it is not affordable, there's nothing transformative about that—that's a copyright violation. In Chapter 3, we will see how to engage in the reasoning process to determine what does (and doesn't) constitute fair use in the context of 21st-century teaching and learning.

Building Consensus Among Educators

With the generous support of the John D. and Catherine T. MacArthur Foundation, I worked with colleagues Peter Jaszi and Pat Aufderheide to bring together groups of educators (from higher education, K–12 settings and youth media organizations) in 10 cities across the United States, including Chicago, Austin, Texas, Philadelphia, Boston, and New York.

After introducing educators to basic concepts in copyright law, we offered them various hypothetical scenarios for discussion, inviting them to reason through the process of determining when educators' or students' use of copyrighted materials was "fair" and "unfair" according to the doctrine of fair use.

As we'll see in Chapter 4, the consensus principles that emerged from these discussions is reflected in the *Code of Best Practices in Fair Use for Media Literacy Education*,[18] which was adopted by several national membership organizations, including the National Association for Media Literacy Education and the National Council of Teachers of English (NCTE), which adopted the *Code* as its official policy in November of 2008. Figure 1.1 shows the organizations that have formally endorsed the *Code*.

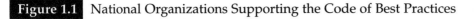

Figure 1.1   National Organizations Supporting the Code of Best Practices

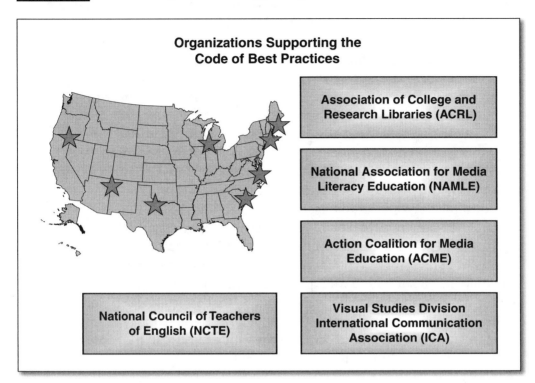

The Code identifies five principles, each with limitations, representing acceptable practices for the fair use of copyrighted materials. It has been carefully reviewed by a distinguished team of legal scholars and copyright lawyers. Educators can:

- make copies of newspaper articles, TV shows, and other copyrighted works, and use them and keep them for educational use;
- create curriculum materials and scholarship with copyrighted materials embedded in them; and
- share, sell, and distribute curriculum materials with copyrighted materials embedded in them.

Learners can:

- use copyrighted works in creating new material; and
- distribute their works digitally if they meet the transformativeness standard.[19]

Nearly every educator finds something unexpected when reviewing this list. When you are used to hearing "No, you can't" when it comes to copyrighted materials, this list can be startling, surprising, and for some, even a little exhilarating. If any of the items on the list were new or unexpected to you, this book will help you discover the myths and misconceptions that you've been holding about copyright and fair use.

What You Can Expect From This Book

The slender size of this book means that it isn't the be-all and end-all of the entire copyright-in-education landscape. It's definitely not one of those copyright books that leaves you feeling more confused after reading than when you started. It's not a book you can use to understand the political history of copyright law, the worldwide challenges surrounding copyright law in a global context, or the shifting implications of copyright for the music business. It's not a book that will help you determine when and how archival copies of copyrighted works can be made. But it is a book that will give you confidence in teaching about copyright and fair use to your students, whether they're in elementary school or graduate school.

This book is simply designed for one purpose: to help educators understand and apply the principles of copyright and fair use to develop students' critical thinking and communication skills.

Maybe you have picked up this book because you're a creator yourself or responsible for distributing creative works. Perhaps you have picked up this book because of your own interests in using digital media, mass media, popular culture, and other copyrighted materials. You want to learn more about how copyright applies to teaching and learning with digital media resources. Perhaps, like me, you've been to a professional-development program where someone passed out a chart that listed all the things you couldn't do with copyrighted works, all the limitations and details, and you thought to yourself, "This just doesn't seem right."

If you're a principal, library media specialist, technology-integration coach, department leader, or curriculum specialist, you may have been asked by your staff or colleagues about a particular situation involving the use (or misuse) of copyrighted material. You may feel some anxiety about what aspects of your own instructional practice are legal and what are not. Or colleagues and friends have told you different, conflicting stories about what fair use means when it comes to education. What are your legal rights to use these materials for teaching and learning?

You already know that when students are engaged in 21st-century learning, they are developing critical thinking, problem solving, creativity, and collaboration skills by using a wide range of media forms and technology tools that connect the classroom to contemporary culture.

The rise of YouTube and social networking sites are creating new opportunities for sharing, commenting upon, and analyzing the ever-changing products of contemporary culture.

But few educational leaders really understand what uses of digital material are protected legally and what's likely to be unlawful. In a cut-and-paste culture, it's only natural to be worried about the array of complex legal and ethical questions that get raised by the widespread use of copyrighted materials by both educators and students.

As we'll see, by understanding how copyright law and the doctrine of fair use apply to your work and the creative work of your students, you can put an end to copyright confusion and be an advocate for promoting a solid understanding of our rights and responsibilities under the law.

Educators sometimes get conflicting messages that may intensify confusion about how copyright law applies to teaching and learning with digital media.

2

Dispelling
Copyright Confusion

A high school English teacher in Chicago named Kate Tabor told a story that's similar to many others I have encountered in schools and colleges around the country, where student creative work is increasingly being forbidden from being screened, shared, or displayed. Her colleague, Mr. Taylor, was an English teacher whose students were reading Shakespeare's *Romeo and Juliet.* He wanted to engage the large number of students whose heads were on their desks or who were simply going through the motions. Mr. Taylor's assignment to his students was unusual: reedit a short image sequence from *The Simpsons* to convey a scene from *Romeo and Juliet.*

As he expected, many of the teen boys in his class went wild over the assignment—with even the most reluctant readers really digging into the play, sticking with the reading, participating in class discussion, eager to find some cool scene they could "Simpsonize." The assignment encouraged students to think carefully about the characters and narrative structure of *Romeo and Juliet.* It created an opportunity to discuss how (and why) *The Simpsons* makes frequent intertextual references to classic works of British and American literature, and it also created an opportunity for students to discover for themselves the challenge of literary adaptation. One thing they learned: It's harder than it looks.

Students addressed Mr. Taylor's unusual assignment in many different ways: One student selected still images of some of the Simpsons characters (for example casting Moe, the bar owner, in the role of Benvolio) with titles scrolling over top recounting the main plot points of Act One. Another student used simple stick animation, with images of Simpsons characters combined with student voice over of Shakespearean lines, so that we see Apu, the convenience store owner, as Paris, saying to Homer, "I do defy thy conjurations, and apprehend thee for a felon here," in the scene where Romeo kills Paris just after Juliet's death.

While unlikely to win prizes at a festival or competition, many students had put substantial effort into their productions and were proud of their work. They had successfully entered into the world of Romeo and Juliet by connecting an unfamiliar text to a familiar one.

But when it came time for sharing this assignment over the school's closed-circuit system, the school's technology coordinator was insistent that the works not be shown. "These works were copyright violations, pure and simple," the administrator claimed.

Sadly, neither Mr. Taylor not Kate Tabor had yet acquired the knowledge and confidence to point out sharing of such work was indeed legal. They didn't understand that the technology coordinator was looking at a chart purporting to tell him the "rules" about fair use, instead of actually understanding the law itself.

SOME KEY TERMS

Copyright is the owner's legal right to reproduce, display, transmit, perform, and modify a work as well as the right to publicly perform a sound recording by digital transmission. A work is automatically copyrighted at the moment of creation, as long as it exists in a fixed, tangible form. You don't have to use the © symbol for a work to be copyrighted. You don't have to register a copyright with the U.S. Copyright Office—although you can if you want to.

An *exemption* is a legal term for an exception to a general rule. Exemptions are generally allowed, not for the benefit of the individual, but for some public advantage. In copyright law, one type of exemption is fair use.

Fair use is the part of copyright law that enables people to make legal use of copyrighted materials *without payment or permission* under some circumstances, especially for uses related to broad and important social goals related to the development of innovation and spread of knowledge, including teaching and learning, scholarship, news reporting, or criticism and commentary.

Public domain is the term used for those works that are no longer copyrighted. The idea behind public domain is noble—it's one way that we freely share the products of our culture with each other. But the public domain has shrunk considerably in recent years. Although copyright is supposed to be a "limited monopoly," new laws have greatly lengthened the terms of copyright protection, so very few works now enter into the public domain.

What Is Copyright?

Copyright is the owner's legal right to reproduce, display, transmit, or modify of work they have created. It's a type of author right. Patent law protects the works of inventors. Together, the works of authors and inventors are called *intellectual property*.[1]

But the term *property* is complicated when it comes to products of the mind because these forms of property are very different from physical property, like cars, clothing, or land.

When I sell or share an item of clothing with my friend, it moves from my closet to her closet. After I have I sold or shared it, it's not in my closet anymore. But when I share information or ideas with you, I will have still have access to them. I haven't lost possession of the ideas when I share them with you. As famous Supreme Court Justice Louis Brandeis explained, "The general rule of law is, that the noblest of human productions—knowledge, truths ascertained, conceptions, and ideas—become, after voluntary communication to others, free as the air to common use."[2]

Who cares about copyright? These days, it seems, everyone cares. When Lawrence Lessig, Stanford Law School professor and author of *Free Culture,* appeared on *The Colbert Report* to talk about his book, *Remix: Making Art and Commerce Thrive in the Hybrid Economy,* it became evident that the topic had moved from the periphery to the mainstream of contemporary culture.[3]

Copyright law reflects the interests of three main types of people who care about it: the individual creators, the publishers or distributors of creative works, and the users or consumers of these works. Of course, there is significant overlap between "owners," "publishers," and "users" because everyone depends on the ability to use other people's work. And with the rise of the Internet, there's often no difference between author and publisher.

Every form of human creativity is connected to and inspired by the works we've come in contact with previously. As Isaac Newton wrote, *"Pigmaei gigantum humeris impositi plusquam ipsi gigantes vident."* It means, "If I have seen further, it is by standing on the shoulders of giants."[4] With the rise of the Internet and other digital technologies, we have been doing a lot of standing on (virtual) shoulders.

Who hasn't found themselves sitting at a computer, transfixed by the remarkable things that can be found there—old films of the musical artists of yesteryear, photographs from every corner of the planet, and games and comics and drawings and stories in forms so unusual that we don't even have generic names or terms for the stuff yet. Every day brings an explosion of materials and forms of expression and communication. The Internet has made intellectual property owners keenly aware of the economic value of media content. And all this copyrighted content floating about means people are naturally using other people's creative ideas in their own work.

COPYRIGHT IN THE CONSTITUTION

Government can establish a copyright system to promote the progress of science and useful arts, by securing for limited times to authors and inventors the exclusive right to their respective writings and discoveries.

—Section 1, Article 8, U.S. Constitution, 1787

The Purpose of Copyright

What's the purpose of copyright? Most people think it protects owners' rights. They think it's about money and profit and control. But looking at the U.S. Constitution, we see that this is not the real purpose of copyright. Carrie Russell explains, "That authors and inventors benefit from copyright is a side effect of encouraging the dissemination of knowledge, and not a direct intent of copyright."[5] As the U.S. Constitution says, the purpose of copyright is to promote the spread of knowledge and innovation.

The intellectual property rights provision of the Constitution was included because the Founders believed that encouraging the development of new ideas and information serves society as a whole.[6] Copyright law promotes this goal through the doctrine of fair use, the part of copyright law that gives rights to those who use the copyrighted materials created by others without payment or permission.

At the heart of copyright law, the doctrine of fair use states that people have a right to use copyrighted materials freely without payment or permission, for purposes such as criticism, comment, news reporting, teaching, scholarship, and research.

Courts realize that educators and students need to use copyrighted materials freely for scholarship, teaching, and learning. In recent years, courts have recognized that when a user of copyrighted materials adds value to, or repurposes materials for a use different from that for which it was originally intended, it will likely be considered fair use. Fair use embraces the modification of existing content if it is placed in new context. As we will see in Chapter 3, such transformative use is at the heart of media literacy education, where

**SECTION 107: THE FAIR USE
DOCTRINE OF THE COPYRIGHT LAW OF 1976**

The fair use of a copyrighted work is not an infringement of copyright. This includes reproduction in copies for purposes such as criticism, comment, news reporting, teaching (including multiple copies for classroom use), scholarship, or research. In determining whether the use made of a work in any particular case is a fair use the factors to be considered shall include:

- the purpose and character of the use, including whether such use is of a commercial nature or is for nonprofit educational purposes;
- the nature of the copyrighted work;
- the amount and substantiality of the portion used in relation to the copyrighted work as a whole; and
- the effect of the use upon the potential market for or value of the copyrighted work.

teachers and students use mass media, popular culture, and digital media to develop critical thinking and communication skills.

The Power of Fair Use

Peter Jaszi explains fair use this way: fair use gives people a right to use copyrighted material when the cost to the copyright holder is less than the social benefit of the use of the copyrighted work. To determine if fair use applies, individuals must assess the specific context and situation concerning the use of a copyrighted work. Hard-and-fast rules are inappropriate, as fair use requires that people use reasoning and judgment.[7]

The fair use doctrine lists four factors: the purpose of the use, the nature of the copyrighted work, the amount used, and the market impact. While some try to turn the four factors into a checklist or flow chart, the courts have repeatedly told us that the four factors cannot be considered in isolation from one another and are not the *only* elements to be considered in making a determination of fair use. In fact, the broad and expansive "four factor" list is deliberate. It is designed to ensure that the concept of fair use is responsive to the wide variety of contexts in which people use other people's copyrighted work in the development of their own work.

In fact, fair use is the safety valve that prevents copyright law from being a form of private censorship. Without fair use, copyright law itself would probably be unconstitutional. Think about it: a law that enables copyright holders to completely control access to information? It sounds like a police state.

How do educators claim fair use? You simply use copyrighted works after making an assessment of the particular context and situation of the specific use of the work. There's nothing formal or official to "do" to claim fair use. You do not have to ask permission or alert the copyright holder when considering the use of materials that are protected by fair use. But, if you choose, you may inquire about permissions and still claim fair use if your request is refused or ignored. In some cases, courts have found that asking permission and then being rejected has actually enhanced fair use claims.

Fair use is explicitly a user right. It gives users the ability to use excerpts from any copyrighted work under some conditions. Fair use enables us to use excerpts even from dominant cultural texts, the ones that are massively popular and produced by huge media companies like Disney, Viacom, and Time Warner. Fair use balances the rights of owners and users in order to fulfill the purpose of copyright.

Figure 2.1 Copyright Supports Both Owners and Users

Copyright Confusion

Most educators make substantial use of copyrighted materials, including newspapers, magazines, films, and Web sites. Now, students can compose and create using multimedia tools they have access to at home and at school. Mac and PC software tools like iMovie, Final Cut Pro, Moviemaker, Photoshop, and Garage Band make it easy for students to create visually and digitally.

WHAT IS CREATIVE COMMONS?

Creative Commons is an alternative licensing scheme, founded by Professor Lawrence Lessig, now at Harvard University Law School, which aims to make it easy for people to build upon other people's work.[8] These licenses allow creators to enable how others can use their work. Many individuals and non-profit organizations have made their work available under these new licenses in order to encourage sharing. People can also make fair use of materials created under a Creative Commons license. But Creative Commons licenses will never be available for a lot of the materials that teachers and students need to use, especially those produced by large commercial media firms.

And these days, students don't need access to expensive software. Free online production tools enable people to create Web pages, edit still or video images, and manipulate sound. For example, Jing (www.jingproject.com) lets you capture moving image sequences from any computer. When students use digital technologies to express themselves in school, they are able to make connections between the culturally familiar world that comes to them through television, the Internet, and other screen media—and the school curriculum's focus on literacy, literature, science, history, social studies, health education, and the arts.

But with the rise of well-publicized file sharing litigation, prominently placed warnings in front of photocopy machines, and those FBI warning labels on DVDs, there has been an increased climate of uncertainty and fear among educators, including those working at the K–12 and university levels. In our report, *The Cost of Copyright Confusion for Media Literacy,* we explored how educators' lack of knowledge and misunderstanding of the law affects teaching and learning. We conducted a series of in-depth interviews with college professors in schools of education and departments of communication, K–12 educators teaching English language arts and social studies, library media specialists, and youth media educators who work in nonprofit organizations.[9]

We discovered, to our chagrin, that copyright confusion affects the spread of innovative instructional practices, limits access to high-quality teaching materials, and perpetuates misinformation.

While some educators are well informed about how issues of copyright and fair use affect their work, many are not. In our in-depth interviews, we discovered that few had any formal training on the subject, and most learned about copyright from informal conversations with colleagues or supervisors.

As Shay Taylor, a teacher at Montgomery Blair High School in Silver Spring, Maryland said, "I heard it from a teacher, who got a memo from another teacher, who read in an e-mail that you could actually get in trouble for using videos in the classroom."[10] Sadly, this is how most educators learn about copyright.

In talking to teachers about their understanding of the law, we found three distinct trends:

1. **See no evil**. *Teachers believe the sky's the limit but fear learning more about copyright.* Some educators believe that they may use any copyrighted materials for any purpose, as long as they identify the source material. Educators generally understand that the materials they employ are usually covered by copyright. But they are often uncertain about the scope of unlicensed use permitted under educational exemptions to copyright, especially under the doctrine of fair use.

Many teachers wrongly believe that fair use entitles them to use any type of copyrighted material for any use as long as it is, broadly speaking, for educational and noncommercial purposes. One teacher said, "With fair use, the sky's the limit."[11] Many teachers wrongly expand the concept of fair use so that it includes any nonprofit application. As one participant explained, "People can use anything they want if they don't make a profit off it."[12] Another teacher explained that fair use enabled him (and his students) to use portions of copyrighted materials as long as the work is cited properly. As we will see in Chapter 3, all of these beliefs are false and inaccurate.

Some educators avoid learning about copyright, believing that an increased understanding of the issues of copyright and fair use might limit the effectiveness of their work. "If I knew what the actual laws were," explained one educator, "I would probably be much more conservative."[13] One educator said, "I've learned not to ask about it."[14] One teacher told us confidently that most American teachers do not have any resources on the topic of copyright outside of the policies their school district may publish.[15] "On this topic, ignorance is bliss,"[16] one educator joked. Of course, this kind of willful ignorance is a significant problem.

2. **Close the door**. *Students and teachers are discouraged from sharing their creative work with the public.* Many teachers use copyrighted materials freely inside their classrooms, believing that they are protected in face-to-face educational settings that may or may not apply when work is exhibited in other venues. One teacher was told by the technology

specialist in her school that her students' media projects could not make any use of copyrighted clips if the program was to appear on the local cable access station in their community. "There is a difference between rules governing work done inside and outside of classroom settings,"[17] explained one educator, who had a misunderstanding of the special protections that are offered to educators under Section 110(1) of the Copyright Act. In many schools, any student work product that incorporates copyrighted materials is kept within the confines of the school. One teacher puts it this way, "The projects my students create tend to stay in the classroom."[18] At a time when it's easier than ever for us to learn and share with each other through the power of online social media, what could be sadder than this statement?

A LIMITED EDUCATIONAL EXEMPTION FOR CLASSROOM INSTRUCTION

Section 110(1) is the part of the Copyright Act of 1976 that allows educators to use "lawfully made" copies of copyrighted materials in the classroom "or similar place devoted to instruction" for educational purposes.

What is a lawfully made copy?

- A photocopy of a printed article
- A school-purchased DVD
- A privately purchased copy of a DVD
- An off-air taped movie
- A rental DVD (from Netflix or Blockbuster)

Section 110(1) is like a narrow layer of extra protection for educators who use print or digital copyrighted materials in face-to-face teaching situations. But we should never interpret the law as saying we can *only* use copyrighted materials in face-to-face teaching situations. For other situations, educators can rely on the doctrine of fair use.

Growing up with the power of the Internet at their fingertips, students now want to speak to a wider audience. Many educators and scholars recognize how composing for an authentic audience can motivate and empower students to do their best work. For many teachers, this simplistic "close the door" policy interferes with creating genuine, meaningful opportunities for learning. It limits the spread of new and innovative instructional practices for K–12 learn-ing at a time when those new ideas are needed more than ever.

3. Hyper-comply. *Some teachers adhere themselves and their students to limits on the use of copyrighted materials that are far more restrictive than the law mandates.* Many teachers are reluctant to share student produc-tions that use copyrighted materials even within a delimited educa-tional network that is specifically designed for educational purposes. One teacher was concerned about a video production his students cre-ate called "Ham Cam." Students videotape in the hallways, where other students inevitably "ham it up." Students then edit together this footage over all different kinds of popular music, in order to explore how the music changes the meaning of the images. "But we don't broadcast these things—not even in our school intranet,"[19] he said.

When it comes to student multimedia festivals and competitions, many programs mandate rules that are far more restrictive than nec-essary under the law. Many of these policies are not educationally sound. They often reflect a fundamental misunderstanding of the law. For example, the 2009 Pennsylvania High School Computer Fair invites students to submit animation projects, video productions, Web sites, and multimedia productions, and it offers cash prizes for outstanding student work. But their copyright policy is confusing, falsely claiming (for example) that "fair use guidelines only apply in educational environments like classrooms or schools." In fact, the greatest number of fair use cases involves for-profit companies being sued by other companies. As we will see in Chapter 3, the doctrine of fair use applies to all citizens, even those who make use of copy-righted materials in their own creative work that they then sell to others.

The Consequences of Copyright Confusion

But even if it is based in a misunderstanding of the law, the anxiety and fear that educators experience is real. Teachers and students have been stymied by school policies that limit their use of taped digital, print, image, and off-air materials.

When we interviewed teachers, we heard many examples of this. One teacher was told by her school librarian that she would be per-sonally liable for copyright violations and the school would not pro-tect teachers if there was a lawsuit.[20] A number of teachers voiced concern about the dampening effect of these policies on the creative use of media and popular culture to promote critical thinking and communication skills.[21] Teachers don't like to think that they have to choose between upholding the law and meeting the educational needs of their students. However, many of the teachers we interviewed felt trapped.

Sadly, misinformation and fear within the publishing industry limits the quality of materials produced. For example, when Deborah Aubert created a media literacy curriculum for Girls, Inc, the nonprofit educational organization, she wanted to help girls develop the skills to wade through the media messages that bombard them. *Girls Get the Message* is a national program that encourages girls and other media consumers to evaluate the messages in media such as television shows, films, CDs, newspapers, Web sites, music videos, magazines, and video games. The program helps girls recognize stereotypes in media and differentiate between those stereotypes and their own lives. Girls learn to "read" media messages with a critical eye as they consider issues of ownership, media business, and the roles of women and minorities "behind the scenes" in media careers.

But in shepherding the program through publication, Aubert discovered that the Girls, Inc attorney was afraid of any reference to copyrighted material appearing in the publication. Aubert explained, "We could not provide people with material or suggest how they obtain material—we could not say 'photocopy' or 'tape.' These restrictions made it difficult for us to be creative."[22]

What is the cost of copyright confusion? Because of the fear of violating copyright, many creative multimedia materials don't get produced and distributed. Teachers make assignments based on their expectation that student media productions will not circulate beyond the classroom, limiting the ability of student work to reach real audiences and address genuine issues of community importance.

Out of misinformation and fear, some educators (at both K–12 and college levels) have discouraged their own students from producing and distributing critical commentaries using video and audio excerpts from commercial media content. Students who do produce critical commentaries of contemporary media have difficulty getting these works submitted to festivals and competitions. As a result, this important work is not shared with broader audiences. The full potential of 21st-century literacy is diminished.

CEASE-AND-DESIST LETTERS

A small number of teachers, scholars, and curriculum producers who have used copyrighted materials in their own creative work have received "cease and desist" letters from media companies. Cease-and-desist letters are inexpensive for media companies to send and they create fear among educators and publishers.

Back in 1992, University of Massachusetts professor Sut Jhally received one of these letters from MTV in response to his educational documentary, *Dreamworlds: Sex, Desire and Power in Rock Video*. He realized it was an attempt to scare him away from creating critical commentary about music videos.

Instead of scaring him, however, it motivated him to create a nonprofit organization, the Media Education Foundation. Now, the company sells over 50 videos on topics including the representation of war in the media, violence in video games, sexism in the media, and many more. Since 1993, he has never been contacted by a media company about the use of their materials in his own creative work. That's because they know he's entitled to use copyrighted materials under the doctrine of fair use.

Fair Use as a User Right

The fair use doctrine is not just for educators—it applies to everyone. It applies to individual, personal uses of copyrighted materials. It allows an individual to make a copy of a lawfully obtained copyrighted work for personal use, for example. Movie fans can make compilations of scenes from their favorite films. Music fans can make compilations—copying favorite songs from their collection to an alternative format.

People also claim fair use whenever they record a TV program using a digital video recorder, copying a program to view at a later time.

Because context and situation determine how fair use applies, we can think of fair use as a "user's right" because without such an exemption the law would be unbalanced, requiring permissions and/or payment in every circumstance, inflating the rights of copyright holders.[23]

In many circumstances, people do not need to ask permission or pay a license fee in order to use a copyrighted work. People must make a fair-use determination by considering the facts of the situation at hand, as fair use requires reasoning and judgment. Copyright confusion comes when people confuse the doctrine of fair use with "educational-use guidelines."

NEGOTIATED AGREEMENTS ON FAIR USE

Have you heard about the 10% rule, or the 30-second rule, or the 45-day rule? These rules come from:

- the 1976 Agreement on Guidelines for Classroom Photocopying in Not-For-Profit Educational Institutions;
- Guidelines for Educational Uses of Music;
- 1981 Guidelines for Off-Air Recording of Broadcast Programming for Educational Purposes; and
- Fair Use Guidelines for Educational Multimedia.

Developed through voluntary negotiations among stakeholders, including lawyers from the world of publishing and various educational organizations, these various "guidelines" are *not* the law.

The Problem With Educational-Use Guidelines

When educators think of fair use, they often are familiar not with the law itself, but with the various sets of so-called "educational-use guidelines" that have been developed by various groups over the past 30 years to provide specificity for interpreting the doctrine of fair use. In fact, from the very beginning, when the lawyers for publishing companies got together with the lawyers from various educational groups to "clarify" fair use, Congress clearly stated that these documents would *not* replace the fair use doctrine and would *not* be included in the actual law. But these efforts persisted, sometimes as a result of industry pressure and sometimes from the perceived need by educators to achieve "certainty" regarding the application of fair use.

Over the past 30 years, the media and publishing industries have used the process of negotiating fair-use guidelines with educational groups, knowing that their lawyers' firepower would overpower the paltry firepower of the educators' legal team. For example, in the mid-1990s, the U.S. Patent and Trademark Office facilitated a series of meetings known as the Conference on Fair Use (CONFU), during which a range of stakeholders (including librarians, educators, media companies, and others) failed to agree about "safe harbors" for various kinds of educational and library uses involving new digital technologies. A related process initiated by the Consortium of College and University Media Centers (CCUMC) produced a set of guidelines for educational multimedia production.

Although the publishing, movie, and record industries happily endorsed these guidelines, they were squarely rejected by the American Library Association, the National Association of State University and Land Grant Colleges, and a coalition of K–12 educators led by the National School Boards Association.

The highly restrictive CCUMC "Proposal for Fair Use Guidelines for Educational Multimedia" sometimes is presented on some Web sites as having the force of law. But it was controversial among both educators and media publishers from the moment it was created. As Columbia University legal scholar Kenneth Crews explains,

> The guidelines bear little relationship, if any, to the law of fair use. The guidelines are negotiated resolutions of conflicts regarding fair use and yet they are often presented as standards to which one must adhere in order to remain within the law.[24]

So, although the educational-use guidelines were designed to be well-meaning efforts to provide additional clarity on the nature of fair use rights, they actually have done more harm than good. For example, in order to pin down and narrow the doctrine of fair use, the guidelines have introduced concepts that aren't even in the law. One of the guidelines refers to *brevity* (achieved by counting the number of words used from an article) and *spontaneity* (making it OK to copy if it is motivated by an instructor's last-minute inspiration, where it would be unreasonable to expect a timely reply to a request for permission). *But these concepts actually are not anywhere mentioned in the law.*

Beware of Charts and Graphs

Because some librarians still equate educational-use guidelines with fair use, various charts have been created that depict the educational-use guidelines in ways that give them the appearance of positive law. However, as Carrie Russell of the American Library Association explained, "In copyright infringement cases, the courts will base their decisions on the law itself, not guidelines."[25]

Whenever you see a chart purportedly depicting copyright and fair use guidelines, you should remember that these depict the negotiated agreements between publishers and some educational groups—they may be helpful in some very limited circumstances, but they do not represent the law and do not have the force of law.

Educational-use guidelines charts can actually distort educators' understanding of the law. When you look at one of the most widely known charts, shown in part in Figure 2.2, nowhere do you see the four factors that are stated in the law.[26] Instead, you see examples of the various negotiated agreements. Here are some of the resultant misunderstandings:

- If you have ever heard of the "rule" that you can use 10% of copyrighted music, or 1,000 words of an essay, or a poem of less than 250 words, or a maximum of 30 seconds of music, or the claim that you can use no more than five images by a single photographer, then you may have confused the educational-use guidelines with the doctrine of fair use.
- If you've heard that you can make an off-air tape of a broadcast program for 45 calendar days after date of recording, but then you must destroy the tape, that comes from one of these negotiated agreements.
- If you've heard that copies can be made only at the request of an individual teacher and may not be regularly recorded in anticipation of requests, you're referring to another one of these negotiated agreements, not the doctrine of fair use.

Many educational-use charts and graphs have legal-sounding orders like, "No broadcast program may be recorded off-air more than once at the request of the same teacher, regardless of the number of times the program may be broadcast." But, don't be fooled. This is not the law. These guidelines are written legalistically in order to achieve their goal: to narrow and pin down the flexible law that is the doctrine of fair use.

Figure 2.2 Beware of Copyright Charts and Graphs: These Charts Are Not the Law

Classroom Copyright Chart

Medium and Material	What You Can Do	The Fine Print
• Poem less than 50 words • Excerpt of 250 words from a poem greater than words • Articles, stories, or essays less than 2,500 words • Excerpt from a longer work (10% of work or 1,000 words, whichever is less, but a minimum of 500 words) • One chart, picture, diagram, graph, cartoon, or picture per book or per periodical issues • Two pages (max) of an illustrated work less than 2,500 words like children's book	• Teachers may make multiple copies for classroom use. • Students may incorporate text in multimedia projects. • Teachers may incorporate into multimedia for teaching courses.	• One copy per student. Use "must be at the instance and inspiration of a single teacher" and when the time frame doesn't allow for asking permission. Nine instances per class per term (newspapers can be used more often). Don't create anthologies. "Consumables" can't be copied. Copying can't be substitute for buying. Copies may be made only from legally acquired originals. • Teachers may keep multimedia for two years; after that, permission is required. Students may keep in portfolio for life.

Hall Davidson's copyright chart is swathed in a royal purple border. It sure looks like it's representing the law. There's rows for print, illustrations and photographs, video, computer software, the Internet and television, and a column that says, "What You Can Do." But the chart is actually just depicting the point of view of the lawyers for the publishing and media industries—and the educational groups who mistakenly thought these guidelines would offer comfort and certainty. It's important to remember that their interpretation of the law is not the law.

Sadly, educational-use guidelines have replaced a genuine understanding of the law for many people, even librarians, lawyers, and information professionals. In a fascinating set of articles from a special issue of the *Journal of the American Society for Information Science* in 1999, scholars discussed the pros and cons of the educational fair-use guidelines. As a legal matter, Mary Levering of the U.S. Copyright Office sees the educational-use guidelines as benign and occasionally helpful. She wrote that the "voluntary guidelines cannot provide an absolute grant of immunity from suit because they do not have the force of law." However, she notes that the guidelines are like "Hints from Heloise," the syndicated column about solving problems like how to remove stains from upholstery or odors from your refrigerator. "Educational fair-use guidelines can serve the same purpose. They save you time and effort, and help you apply copyright principles more easily and quickly."[27]

But in that same special issue of the journal, other experts viewed the guidelines as truly dangerous to education. Those words are not hyperbole—there is real concern that the educational-use guidelines will damage the practice of education. Library science scholar Kenneth Frazier of the University of Wisconsin–Madison believes that educational fair-use guidelines "betray our historical commitment to open access to information."[28]

Commercial publishers and media companies like these guidelines because they help reduce fair use to minimal uses that are defined, controlled, and determined by copyright owners. But negotiated fair-use guidelines are never neutral interpretations of the law. According to Frazer, they are "grounded in legal theories that fundamentally change the concept of fair use in education to the economic advantage of publishers and database owners."[29]

Fair Use and the Marketplace

Some educators mistakenly believe that the doctrine of fair use only applies when there is no commercial market for licensing a particular work. They believe that you can claim fair use unless the publisher or media company has a system in place for paying for the use of the material. If there is a system in place for paying, some educators believe they (and their students) *always* have to pay. But that's not true.

Just because there's a licensing system in place (for images, for video, for music, for online access to newspaper articles, or whatever) doesn't mean that you always, in all situations, must pay the license fee. Even when there is a license system available, you still have the right to claim fair use.

There are some companies that exploit the ignorance of American educators as it relates to this topic. Some media industry lawyers claim that fair use only exists because society has not (yet) discovered a way to commodify every single type of copyrighted work. Fortunately, as we will see in Chapter 3, people can claim fair use even when well-established for-profit licensing schemes are in place.

The doctrine of fair use has always allowed American citizens to exercise rights to use copyrighted works for private, noncommercial purposes, with or without a market context. In a democratic society, the exclusive rights of publishers are balanced with the legitimate needs of the public for reasonable and affordable access to information.

Copyright, Fair Use, and Online Learning

Recently, it seems like media industry lobbyists have been effective in their efforts to narrow the scope of fair use when it applies to digital media. For example, the 2002 TEACH Act allows educators to use digital materials for distance education, but it limits and narrows educators' rights, creating a real gap between what's allowed in face-to-face teaching and what's permitted for distance education.

As we learned, Section 110(1) of the Copyright Act gives educators broad freedom to use lawfully made copies of movies, music, and images in face-to-face educational settings. The 2002 TEACH Act added Section 110(2), which provides 22 different limitations and prerequisites to consider when using digital resources under this particular exemption. Resource B, at the back of this book, contains excerpts from copyright law that apply to educators.

For example, the law forces educational institutions making use of digital materials to use technological measures that prevent retention of the work for longer than a class session. Unfortunately, the law also establishes a narrow definition of what constitutes an educational setting. The TEACH Act applies only when the educational use of content is "an integral part of a class session offered as a regular part of the systematic mediated instructional activities of a governmental body or an accredited nonprofit educational institution."[30] Further, the content must be for the sole use of "students officially enrolled in the course for which the transmission is made."[31]

The TEACH Act put artificial limits on what can be shared, requiring that the use of copyrighted content must be "directly related" to the teaching content. Materials that are ancillary or supportive, but not directly related to a lesson, may not be shared. Materials must be in the "amount comparable to what is typically displayed in the course of a live classroom session."[32] So, those of us who want our college students to view a two-hour documentary film, as homework, so that we can use our one-hour of classroom time more productively for discussion, might be stymied by this law.[33]

As William Fisher and William McGeveran of the Berkman Center for Internet and Society at Harvard Law School point out, the references to class sessions, accredited institutions, and official enrollment make it clear that legislators imagined the TEACH Act applying only to endeavors that resemble traditional classroom instruction in every possible way, except that they occur through digital technology such as the Internet.[34]

Under this new provision of the law, the use of copyrighted materials is clearly not protected for teachers in an adult-literacy class offered by a nonprofit but unaccredited institution. Many other settings and contexts will not be covered under the TEACH Act. This creates concern among educators who use copyrighted materials to teach in nonprofit afterschool organizations, summer camps, and other informal education settings.

COPYRIGHT EDUCATION MATERIALS ALWAYS HAVE A POINT OF VIEW

Curriculum is never neutral. Looking at one sample of a learning objective, can you spot which of these educational materials represent the point of view of corporate media industries?

Copyright Alliance

Sample Learning Objective: to help students recognize that duplicating software and other copyrighted material is illegal and unfair to others.

Electronic Frontier Foundation

Sample Learning Objective: to clarify the difference between legitimate creative uses versus infringement of copyrighted material by accurately identifying the scope and limits of copyright law.

Media Education Lab at Temple University

Sample Learning Objective: to recognize that ideas about copyright are in transition as a result of changes in communication technologies.

Motion Picture Association of America and Weekly Reader

Sample Learning Objective: to show students about the harms of copying DVDs and the penalties for illegally downloading movies from the Internet.

There's one bit of good news: Educators who find Section 110(2) too limiting can still rely on fair use, which permits reasonable uses of digital materials like movies, music, and images for both local and remote students.

Industry-Sponsored Copyright Misinformation

The copyright misinformation that's available online is simply staggering. When you Google "fair use and education," you're likely to stumble across a Web site developed by a teacher named Cathy Newsome in 1997. This misinformation is presented in an attractive, easy-to-digest format. With simple graphics that feature a chalkboard and apple, the Web site presents the educational-use guidelines as law. The information on this Web site comes from the most controversial of all the educational-use guidelines, the CCUMC guidelines.

But other kinds of copyright education materials are even more insidious. When teens use the Microsoft Mybytes.com, Microsoft's music mixing Web site, teens can build songs and then share them as full MP3 downloads or ringtones. But as Joseph Wilk of the Young Adult Library Services Association explains,

> It's hard not to notice an agenda to the Mybytes site, which immerses teens in the concept of intellectual property rights. They hear statements from artists about how glad they are for laws which protect them from consumer piracy and plagiarism and canned video clips featuring soundbites from teens on intellectual property rights. And just like when the dairy industry has a hand in the food pyramid, are these the people from whom teens are going to get a healthy understanding of intellectual property?[35]

The music and media industries have created copyright education materials that represent their interests and, in the process, misinform teachers and students about their actual legal rights.

These days, commercially sponsored copyright curriculum materials are increasingly visible. For example, the Copyright Alliance is a copyright activist group that represents the interests of the music and media industries. Its members include NBC, News Corporation, and other large media companies. They have copyright lessons for teachers and students. However, when you visit their Web site, you might not recognize that this group has a distinct point of view on the topic of copyright. But the Copyright Alliance ignores the concept of fair use and advocates a move to a "permissions-based" culture and positions all unauthorized copying as theft.[36]

When you watch the animated video at the Copyright Clearance Center (which is a for-profit company that handles the permissions process for the publishing industry), it's no surprise that the video tells you that fair use is "uncertain" and "difficult"—and that's why you should always ask permission and pay license fees for every copyrighted work you use.[37]

This point of view is common among people in the media industry, and who can blame them? From their point of view, fair use is a pesky devil of a law that interferes with their profits.

Media industries could make much more money if the doctrine of fair use disappeared. If people always had to pay every time they used a work, educational institutions would have to pay a lot more than they do already for resources and materials. The Internet would be more like a crazy department store where if you touch it, you buy it. Libraries would disappear. That would be a goldmine. Their solution: Use persuasive techniques to change people's understanding of the law.

Step one: Equate sharing with stealing. If everyone believes that all forms of sharing are illegal, then eventually fair use will wither away. After all, when it comes to rights, it's always a "use it or lose it" proposition. Here's the way Weekly Reader Custom Publishing president Terry Bromberg, whose organization created materials on behalf of the Motion Picture Association of America, explains it, "By teaching students about copyright protection, we can educate them on what constitutes stealing."[38]

So, beware of the many copyright education materials that distort the law to suit business interests. One of the primary motivations behind this book is to counter these kinds of biased and wrongheaded perceptions that profoundly misrepresent the law. Of course, this book has a point of view, too. This book's point of view: *Educators must gain knowledge and use the legal rights granted to them (and their students) under the doctrine of fair use, part of the Copyright Law of 1976.*

Let's be clear: Everyone, including copyright owners, is entitled to tell their story. Of course, copyright owners (generally not the "authors" of creative material) have got far bigger budgets and far bigger megaphones than those whose approach to copyright education includes the doctrine of fair use. For example, the Motion Picture Association of America talked the Boys Scouts into developing a copyright merit badge that conveys the industry perspective. The Recording Industry Association of America has produced a video that tells students to be skeptical of free content, explaining (falsely) that it's always illegal to make a copy of a song.

On the other hand, the copyright lesson plans my colleagues and I created at the Media Education Lab (www.mediaeducationlab.com) emphasize how fair use applies to the work of teachers and students who use copyrighted materials in building students' critical thinking and communication skills. The Electronic Frontier Foundation, a nonprofit civil-rights organization concerned with digital rights, also has a copyright education Web site (www.teachingcopyright.org), which emphasizes people's rights to share information using digital technology.

How can you identify a Web site that might have inaccurate information about your rights? Look carefully at how they define or refer to the doctrine of fair use.

- In the Copyright Alliance's 12-minute video for teachers, the phrase "fair use" is never even mentioned.
- At the Copyright Clearance Center, fair use is referred to with terms like "confusing," "uncertain" or "vague." Those words signal a dismissive attitude towards fair use.
- If seeking permission is presented as the first and most desirable option, look at the interests of the author, and consider how their interests intersect with the topic.

Since all messages are constructed, it's critically important to identify the author, purpose and point of view of the messages we receive. That's a key concept of media literacy education. Curriculum materials are never neutral—they always come with a point of view attached.

Educators need to examine copyright curriculum materials to make sure that they reflect the best interests of the public and not just the private interests of large media corporations.

Imagine how the future of education would be diminished if every time information were used or shared formal permission or license fees were required. It's not the kind of future I want for America—it would exacerbate even further the huge inequities that exist between schools serving the wealthy and those who serve the poor and working class. Fair use is central to the practice of teaching and learning. It's that simple.

Whether we see no evil, close the door, or hyper-comply with rules that are far more restrictive than the law mandates, copyright confusion impairs the quality of teaching and learning. Copyright confusion limits the scope of innovation in education just at a time when new online technologies are making new forms of knowledge sharing easier than ever. Now that we understand that the educational-use guidelines cannot be understood as law and cannot be confused with the doctrine of fair use, it's time to turn to Chapter 3, so we can dig in and better understand how fair use applies to the practices of teaching and learning for the 21st century.

The doctrine of fair use supports the work of educators who are exploring new instructional practices that involve accessing, analyzing, and composing using a range of digital texts, tools, and technologies.

3

Users Have Rights, Too

Sarah Sutter, a photography teacher at Wiscasset High School in rural Maine, is exploring how to use social media to promote learning—and in the process, she is running into questions about copyright. She is working with Youth Voices (www.youthvoices.net) to connect her students to students at a school in New York City who are also studying photography.

These days, educators at all levels are exploring how to use the Internet and social media tools for teaching and learning. A wave of innovative instructional practices by educators from many disciplines and fields is creating new questions about the educational use of copyrighted materials. Now, the work products of both teachers and students are increasingly visible in online environments that are shared, collaborative, and (more or less) public.

At the Youth Voices Web site, students can post their own writing online and read the work of others from many different high schools around the nation. The Digital Photography Group is part of Youth Voices where students and their teachers share, distribute, and discuss photography.

At the Web site, student-to-student conversations, collaborations, and civic actions are nurtured through writing about current events, creating multimedia productions as part of course assignments, and responding to copyrighted videos, images, or music. Students are encouraged to read the writing of their peers and respond to it, creating a community of readers and writers who share creative work online.

In one activity, Sarah Sutter, Susan Ettenheim of the New York City Writing Project, and Chris Sloan, who teaches English, media, and photography at Judge Memorial Catholic High School in Salt Lake City Utah, worked collaboratively to have their students compare and contrast the work of famous photographers, using Google Docs to share their PowerPoint slides with each other.[1] Each student selects two photographers to compare and contrast. This gives students an opportunity to learn more about each photographer and recontextualize the artist's work in light of their own learning.

As part of the process, students embed their slides within the Youth Voices Web site, where other students can comment, ask questions, and share ideas. The assignment includes the opportunity to compare and contrast photographers including Lewis Hine and Jacob Riis, Margaret Bourke White and Henri Cartier Bresson, and many others, including the work of contemporary photographers like Abelardo Morell.

But Sarah and her collaborating teachers have had some questions about whether they could (or could not) post these slides online at the Youth Voices Web site. The students' slides included examples from the work of famous photographers, whose work was protected by copyright. Could they be placed online for anyone to see? Would that be a violation of copyright? Sarah and her colleagues just weren't certain. They decided to post them online and invited students to comment on them, but they did so with some trepidation. Does the students' uses of copyrighted images in their online slide presentations constitute a fair use, or does their work violate copyright?

New Instructional Practices Proliferate

Many instructional practices are now becoming more widespread in the context of K–12 teaching and learning where issues of copyright and fair use are relevant:

- The use of digital files, presentation slides, videos, and audio clips as part of classroom teaching.
- Teaching about mass media, popular culture, and digital media using copyrighted works.
- The use of online networks for teachers that enable the sharing of ideas and resource materials.
- Student use of copyrighted materials within their own creative and academic work, including images, quotes from print material, and excerpts from videos, Web sites, music, presentations, podcasts, and wikis.
- The use of social networking spaces where students can share resources, engage in dialogue, post, and discuss ideas.

- The use of online software tools for creative expression, like Flickr and Voicethread, that blend media production with the power of social media.
- Formal or informal online learning environments where students and teachers engage in learning.

In talking with Sarah and her colleagues about the digital photography project in a Teachers Teaching Teachers (www.teachersteaching teachers.org) podcast, Peter Jaszi addressed questions about the legal status of this work. But he did not offer legal advice. When teachers asked him, "Can these slides be posted online?" Peter responded,

> The fair use doctrine is a much more flexible and powerful tool than it is given credit for. What makes a use fair—what makes an unlicensed use without payment or permission legal—isn't so much the context of the use, but the nature of the use.

Jaszi explained that much depends on the answer to the question, "What has that student done with the copyrighted material?"[2]

The key that unlocks the doctrine of fair use is the idea of transformativeness—that is, has the user added value or repurposed the work? Instead of relying on lawyers, librarians, or school administrator to tell us what is and what is not fair use, educators and students need to make that determination for themselves. That's what the copyright law both permits and requires.

In this chapter, I review an important legal case that has established the concept of transformative use as a way to understand the doctrine of fair use, and then I return to Sarah's students and their use of the work of famous photographers. We will consider how copyright applies to one common instructional approach used in 21st-century literacy and learning: the student-created online slide presentation. But first, let's explore some basic principles about the relationship between copying and creativity.

The Political and Educational Value of Copying

Copying has gotten a bad rap. Some people see copying as the antithesis of creativity. But actually, copying is part of the creative process. It's simply impossible to do anything creatively without making reference to the work of other creative products. It's a truism

USING SOMEONE ELSE'S WORDS

Many forms of advocacy and action involve acts of communication that make use of other people's words and ideas. It's how we signal our alliance with others who share our beliefs.

For example, political advocacy groups encourage citizens to send letters to their Congressional representatives, copying a fill-in-the-blank form with specific phrases and ideas that indicate a particular political opinion. When political leaders see the same phrases and ideas coming in from many constituents, they respond.

Even though our culture values originality of expression, in the real world sometimes the best way to send a message is to use someone else's words.

to say that writers, musicians, and artists inevitably borrow from other writers, musicians, and artists.

But copying is part of many kinds of creative production. I copy the recipe I read in the newspaper, modifying it and adapting it based on what's in my pantry and refrigerator. Young lovers copy lines of poetry to give to the admired one, modifying and adding their own thoughts along with those of the poet. Some share mix tapes with friends, selecting, sequencing, and organizing music to send a specific message, to share their feelings and ideas about life.

Leaders have always borrowed ideas to communicate effectively with a mass audience. Martin Luther King's "I Have a Dream" speech made use of the Declaration of Independence, the Bible, the work of other preachers, song lyrics from "America," and the spiritual "Free at Last." According to legal scholar Rebecca Tushnet, persuaders of all sorts often make use of copying simply because it's rhetorically effective to do so.[3] The use of borrowed material has long been understood as a highly effective component of persuasive and political communication. For example, when Martin Luther King used words his listeners had already heard, he connected his own message to ideas that they already believed. For this reason, we often see copying in advertising, religious, and political discourse.

Similarly, in education, copying is recognized as a part of the learning process and has always been used as an educational tool. Children studying the life of young George Washington know that, like other boys of the time period, he maintained a series of copybooks, where he reproduced all manner of business and legal papers as well as memorable quotations about life, love, and social manners.

In many disciplines and fields all over the world, copying is a part of learning. In the world of art education, there's considerable consensus about copying as a means to develop skills of artistic expression. As art educator Paul Duncum explains, "Through copying, children acquire the graphic schemata necessary for representation." In both art and literacy education, copying, as a part of the learning process, contributes to the development of skills like flexibility and synthesis.[4]

When learning to write, learners imitate the sentence structure of preexisting written works in order to understand and master more complex syntactical forms. As part of learning the composition process, we use and rework the sentences of others to learn how they expressed their ideas and to learn how to build upon their ideas to create our own.

Authorship and the Romantic Ideal

Educators may adhere to beliefs about authorship and creativity that limit their understanding of both copyright and the creative process. Peter Jaszi has explained that the concept of "authorship" is an artifact of the marketplace—it developed historically in relation to the growth of culture as an industry, around the time of the Enlightenment.[5]

One of the most romantic of beliefs is the idea of the sole author, the genuinely creative individual whose work springs from "nature." When I think of the concept of the sole author, it's Emily Dickinson who comes to mind—isolated, sick, and secluded Emily who tossed her 1,800 bizarre little poems into a drawer in her garret on the top floor of her family's house in Amherst, Massachusetts.

As an English major at the University of Michigan, I read poems by Emily Dickinson, whose work consists of highly original and psychologically complex poems exploring themes of loss, death of self, and nature. (My professors never informed me about the nasty, protracted copyright dispute between her heirs and her editors. In the Romantic conceptualization of authorship, issues of markets and money are simply not discussed.) Only much later did I discover that the poems themselves were heavily edited by her mentor and friend, Thomas Wentworth Higginson, who altered the unusual punctuation and other features of the strange little poems when publishing her works. For seven years, he worked without pay to bring the most popular Dickinson texts to press, making editorial changes that helped the poems to be more accessible and more meaningful to readers.[6]

The "sole author" narrative is mostly a by-product of the Enlightenment and its conceptualization of creativity, rooted in the concept of the individual. With all the collaboration and teamwork that is at the heart of the information age, it is truly ironic that we continue to hold on to these narratives of authorship, the ones that emphasize genius and singular accomplishment.

Today, nearly all forms of contemporary creative expression involve collaboration and teamwork. For example, this book is the result of a multiyear collaboration between Patricia Aufderheide, Peter Jaszi, and myself. Most new ideas develop as a result of the conversation process and the sharing of ideas.

Writers in many professions, including medicine, science, and engineering, generally work in teams. When they document their work in writing, there are multiple authors. In fact, in the professional fields, the "authors" of a work sometimes are not the writers of the work. Authorship is often granted for the provision of funding, the collection of data, preparation of statistical analysis, and preparation of tables and graphics. While in the 1950s most scholarly and professional writing was done by sole authors, today most writing is done by a team, working together.

When K–12 educators focus exclusively on the idea of "doing your own work," it actually undercuts the development of important skills that are necessary for collaboration and teamwork in contemporary society.

We need to reflect on our assumptions about the creative process when considering the legitimate role of copying in the development of new ideas.

Although we'll take up the issue of plagiarism and attribution (citing sources and offering credit to the works we use) in Chapter 4, it's wise not to view copying through the narrow lens of "pirating" or "stealing" or any other simplistic or artificial metaphors. The doctrine of fair use, which is an essential component of the Copyright Act of 1976, exists to support the kinds of copying, borrowing, and sharing that are so essential to fertilize and nurture the creative process.

Understanding Transformative Use

To understand how the doctrine of fair use protects creativity, the case of *Bill Graham Archives v. Dorling Kindersley* (DK) is especially useful and clear. This case is *not* about teachers or students, so it's not about the meaning of fair use in a specifically nonprofit educational context. It features a commercial book publishing company being sued by a copyright owner.

But, this case has a lot of relevance to the ways that teachers and students use copyrighted materials for teaching and learning—and because it helps elucidate the concept of transformativeness, it's especially useful to teachers who are involved in having students create or compose new materials that may make use of copyrighted works, including images. It is also a great story of how the law actually works.

In October of 2003, DK published *Grateful Dead: The Illustrated Trip*[7] in collaboration with Grateful Dead Productions. The giant, heavy, full-color coffee table book tells the story of the Grateful Dead along a timeline running continuously through the book. Many people recognize the band, which was known for its eclectic style that incorporated many musical genres including rock, folk, bluegrass, blues, reggae, country, and jazz. They were legendary for their unique, live improvisational performances. Tapes of their live performances, created by audience members, circulated freely among the network of fans and increased the demand for their work.

The book itself uses over 2,000 images representing dates in the Grateful Dead's history, with short text boxes about specific topics including details of the life of Jerry Garcia, the band's lead guitarist. Each page features a collage of images, text, and graphic art designed to both entertain and inform the reader, in the manner of all books published by Dorling Kindersley.

When preparing the book for publication, the folks at DK contacted Bill Graham Archives to get permission to reproduce seven poster and concert ticket images. Bill Graham Archives (now called Wolfgang's Vault) owns one of the world's largest collections of original concert posters, featuring hundreds of rock posters, political posters, and sports posters. The Archives wanted to charge the publisher an exorbitant fee—from the point of view of the folks at DK, the license terms that Bill Graham Archives wanted were ridiculously restrictive.

So instead of paying the fee, DK proceeded with publication of *Illustrated Trip* anyway, reproducing seven images originally depicted on Grateful Dead event posters and tickets without payment or permission for the use of the copyrighted material. When Bill Graham Archives sued DK for copyright infringement, the publisher responded that their use of the copyrighted work constituted a fair use under the Copyright Act of 1976.

The U.S. District Court for the Southern District of New York first ruled that the publisher's unlicensed reproduction of the images was indeed a fair use of copyrighted material. When Bill Graham Archives continued to press the case, the Second Circuit Court (one level below the Supreme Court) reaffirmed the decision, ruling in favor of the book publisher on May 9, 2006. As it turned out, Dorling Kindersley did not have to ask permission or pay a license fee to use the images from the Bill Graham Archives since they were using the materials under the doctrine of fair use.[8]

So, let's explore. Why was DK's use of the copyrighted images *not* a violation of copyright?

As you remember from Chapter 2, fair use involves a case-by-case analysis of the context and situation of the unlicensed use of copyrighted work. Four factors to consider are (1) the purpose and character of the use, (2) the nature of the copyrighted work, (3) the amount and substantiality of the portion used in relation to the copyrighted work as a whole, and (4) the effect of the use upon the potential market for or value of the copyrighted work. As the courts have told us, there may be other factors to consider as well. In this case, the court had to consider whether the DK book is "transformative" in nature in order to determine whether its claim of fair use was justified.

Essentially, the judge asks: Does the new work merely supersede the objects of the original creation, or instead does it add something new, with a further purpose or different character, altering the first with new expression, meaning, or message? As one judge put it, *"The*

Figure 3.1   An Example of Transformative Use

The purpose of the original: to generate publicity for a concert.

The purpose of the new work: to document and illustrate the concert events in historical context.

ultimate test of fair use . . . is whether the copyright law's goal of promoting the progress of science and useful arts would be better served by allowing the use than by preventing it."[9]

To determine whether the use of copyrighted material is a fair use, take a look at Figure 3.1. Let's consider the genre and purpose of the original material and the new use of the material. In this case, the original poster images are persuasive in nature, while the book is a biographical work. The posters themselves had two purposes: artistic expression and promotion. The posters were designed to attract interest and persuade people to buy concert tickets. In contrast, DK used these images in the book for a different purpose—as historical artifacts. In the publication, the small images of the posters help depict the concert events featured in the book's timeline. The publisher's use of images placed in chronological order on a timeline in a book is different from the mere expressive and commercial use of images on concert posters or tickets.

Because the works are displayed to commemorate historic events, arranged in a creative fashion, and displayed in significantly reduced form, the court held in favor of the fair use claim.

Even though Bill Graham Archives had a licensing system in place for charging fees for the use of their work, this did not mean that they could financially control the transformative use of their copyrighted materials. The Second Circuit Court judge wrote,

> In a case such as this, a copyright holder cannot prevent others from entering fair use markets merely "by developing or licensing a market for parody, news reporting, educational or other transformative uses of its own creative work." Moreover, a publisher's willingness to pay license fees for reproduction of images does not establish that the publisher may not, in the alternative, make fair use of those images.[10]

So, just because the *New York Times* has a system in place for charging educators for the use of newspaper articles doesn't mean that you can't use newspaper articles freely for educational purposes under the doctrine of fair use. Just because a photojournalist charges a newspaper for the use of his images doesn't mean you can't use an image you find in a newspaper as inspiration for your own creative artwork that you then sell on the open market. Fair use is designed to promote all forms of creativity.

Essentially, this case establishes that the doctrine of fair use is not just applicable to educational and noncommercial works, but it also applies to a wide range of creative works that make fair use of copyrighted materials—and are designed for the commercial marketplace.

Interpreting Transformativeness

Transformativeness is perhaps not an all-or-nothing concept—it may be a matter of degree. The concepts of audience, meaning, and interpretation can be useful in legal analysis, says Laura Heymann,[11] who explains how a careful look at audience interpretation can be useful for determining the degree of transformative use of a copyrighted work.

She uses the concept of *discursive community*, the group of people who are participating in the process of interpreting any particular work. Heymann argues that when a new use of copyrighted material provides a new meaning or interpretation of the work that is significant enough to create a distinct and separate discursive community around the second work, the use is more likely to be transformative.[12] This concept could be of use to judges in making fair use decisions.

For example, the meaning of a Jacob Riis photograph printed in an early 20th-century newspaper (reaching a general audience) is significantly different from the meaning of the use of that photo in an art history journal (which reaches an audience of scholars), which is different from the meaning created by its inclusion in a rap music video (which reaches an audience of rap music fans). Context and situation determine how fair use applies.

Transformativeness in K–12 Education

Two questions emerge when considering whether a specific use of copyrighted materials is a fair use:

TRANSFORMATIVENESS IN K-12 EDUCATION

1. Did the unlicensed use "transform" the material taken from the copyrighted work by using it for a different purpose than that of the original, or did it just repeat the work for the same intent and value as the original?

2. Was the material taken appropriate in kind and amount, considering the nature of the copyrighted work and of the use?

If the answers to these two questions are yes, a court is likely to find a use fair. Such uses of copyrighted material are not likely to be challenged by copyright owners.

But because fair use requires reasoning and interpretation, each case is different, and it is important to look at the particulars of the situation and context in some detail.

At the beginning of the chapter, we introduced the work of Sarah Sutter, a photography teacher from Maine, and her colleagues from New York and Utah, whose students are using copyrighted materials in their own creative work as part of their photography class. They share their work with students from other schools and comment on each others' work.

We don't want to use a checklist or formula to determine fair use—we learned in Chapter 2 about the dangers of that kind of thing. So let's take a careful look at the assignment described at the opening of the chapter and consider the context and situation of the use to see whether or not the doctrine of fair use applies.

Comparing and Contrasting Photographs: An Online Production Project

Overview

Students compare and contrast two famous photographers and create an online slide presentation to share their work with students in other parts of the country. This assignment was developed by Sarah Sutter, Susan Erdenheim, and Chris Sloan (who are all affiliated with the National Writing Project), and the work is posted online at Youth Voices (www.youthvoices.net).

Purpose and Character of the Use

Let's consider the instructional process and learning objectives. To meet the demands of the assignment's criteria, students have to gain familiarity with the majority of work produced by the two photographers they are comparing and contrasting. The teacher encourages students to look at earlier work as well as later work in addition to images they are famous for. After looking at the artists' work, the lesson invites students to explore these questions:

- How are these two artists' styles the same?
- What elements do they use in a similar manner?
- How are they different?

Students are encouraged to learn more about the techniques of shooting they use: what kind of camera, film or glass plate negatives, what kind of positives—gelatin silver paper, platinum, albumen, calotype, or other media. There is some deadline pressure: Students have only three class periods to work on the assignment, which includes the process of gathering information and creating a presentation using Google Docs. Figure 3.2 shows an example of the slides created and posted online by Beau Imhoff, a student who completed the assignment.

Students are also required to use a citation format to identify the photographic work they use in their slide presentations. They identify the photographer's name, the date the image was created, and the title, as well as the URL where the image was located online. After work has been posted, students review the work of their peers to learn more about other photographers and to offer feedback about their work. Metacognitive processing is also encouraged—students reflect on their own work as photographers, responding to questions like these:

- What can you learn from these famous photographers?
- What did they try that you would like to learn?
- What did they do that you never even thought about trying?

Figure 3.2 Student Photo Assignment: Compare and Contrast

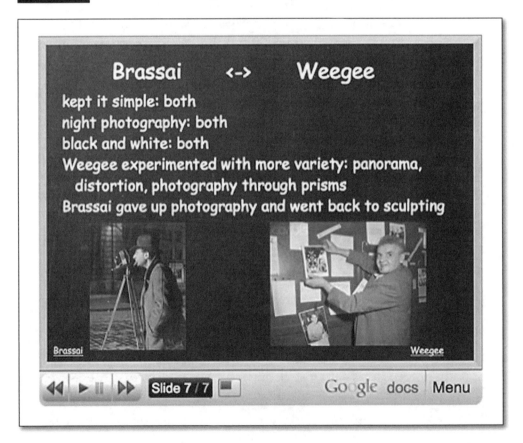

- What did they do that makes you feel like kindred spirits?
- What do you admire?
- How will seeing and knowing this photographer's work affect you and your work?

And here are some of the learning goals:

- Develop a deeper appreciation for the historical context of photography as an artistic discipline.
- Learn more about the works of two important photographers and the various genres, themes, and styles of photography as an art form.
- Strengthen research skills, especially accessing and using information.
- Strengthen analysis and composition skills in the creative use of language and images.
- Promote expressive communication in a collaborative online environment.

Sarah Sutter and her teaching colleagues believe there is significant educational value to posting student work online—such sharing creates an authentic audience by enabling students in rural Maine, Utah, and New York City to exchange perspectives.

Nature of the Work and Amount and Substantiality Used

One important quality of photographs is that, in almost all cases, users will need to reproduce the entire work—not an excerpt or a portion. The famous photographers whose work is used in this assignment created their work for a variety of purposes, including to inform, to persuade, for self-expression, and to make money. To complete this assignment, students find online reproductions of the photos, available on the Web sites of nonprofit foundations, educational institutions, or in some cases, online galleries where work is available for sale. For example, a student who is writing about the work of Henri Cartier Bresson, the French photographer who is often considered the father of modern photojournalism, may access image thumbnails at the After Image Gallery, an online photography dealer. The student may also download Bresson portraits at the Web site of the National Portrait Gallery, part of the Smithsonian Museum. Or, the student may find and use examples of his photography at Magnum Photos, the famous commercial photo agency. At Magnum, these high-quality digital images contain the watermark of the agency, protecting the work from illegal reproduction.

Depending on the particular nature of the lesson or activity, a student may need to use different types of image reproductions. For some assignments, a high-quality image may be necessary; in other cases, a thumbnail will do just fine. In any case, the doctrine of fair use applies.

WHAT IS A DIGITAL WATERMARK?

A **watermark** is a visible or invisible image, which appears on some forms of digital media, including images, audio, or video files. It is a dimension of digital rights management. A digital code identifies the file's copyright information. If the signal is copied, then the information is also carried in the copy. With some digital watermarking technology, software can be used that will track online copies, informing the photographer of the Web sites where a particular image is used. A photographer may track the use of her images and send a letter to the user about the use of her material.

However, no technology can determine whether or not a particular use of copyrighted material is a fair use. Fair use always requires interpretation and reasoning by humans. We would never want technology to replace or reduce our rights in any way.

Looking at the student work shown on Figure 3.2, we see that the student has used images depicting Brassai and Weegee, two 20th-century European photojournalists who specialized in street photography, capturing images of urban life. This particular student project consists of seven slides that describe and analyze the work of each photojournalist, culminating with a comparison–contrast. In this case, the student has chosen a blackboard motif, symbolizing education. When an image is shown, there is a hyperlink provided back to the source of the image. In an analysis of fair use, it is important to consider the specific choices made by the new user to *add value or repurpose* the original. The student's purpose in using these images is to fulfill the requirements of the class assignment and accomplish the learning objectives identified above. This is clearly a different purpose than the original creation of these images.

When we examine where students located digital copies of images, it's clear that they often used secondary sources, places where others have already uploaded these images as part of *their* creative work. For example, the bibliography offered by Mariel Hernandez and Andrea Palma, two high school students who created a comparison–contrast project about the photographers Jacob Riis and Louis Hine, includes reference to a WordPress blog, a Blogspot blog, and the History Matters Web site, created by the American Social History Project at the City University of New York and George Mason University. Educators can use student performance on assignments like this to assess the development of students' research skills.

Effect on Market

Does this use of the copyrighted materials substantially affect the market for the original? We must ask about whether the distribution of copyrighted content embedded in a student slide presentation infringes the rights of the copyright holder. Is student work of this type in competition with the market for artistic photography? It's a judgment call. Evidence would need to be provided to determine that there was a negative effect on sales.

It's fair to ask the question, What if many students in photography classes all over the country were completing this type of assignment? Would that have a negative effect on the market? Because copyright law supports the goals of creativity and the spread of knowledge, the more strongly transformative a new creative work is, the less the issue of economic harm matters. New works—created from the fair use of copyrighted materials—naturally create new markets. But when works are created using copyrighted materials and have only a small degree of transformativeness, then it's right that we look critically at whether the new work could serve *as a substitute for the original.* Such works may be infringing.

It's important to note that we don't need to worry about whether a parody or negative review impairs the market for the original. As I explained earlier, copyright law cannot be used to protect a copyrighted work from criticism, even if the criticism negatively affects sales. Copyright law should never be used as a form of private censorship. The question of market impact needs to be considered in some depth to appreciate how copyright and the doctrine of fair use actually promote creativity and the spread of knowledge.

Now, it's time for each reader to make a fair-use determination: Is this a fair use of copyrighted work? Did the unlicensed use transform the material taken from the copyrighted work by using it for a different purpose than that of the original, or did it just repeat the work for the same intent and value as the original? Was the material taken appropriate in kind and amount, considering the nature of the copyrighted work and of the use?

Fair use is not the kind of concept where there is one "right" and one "wrong" answer, until a case gets in front of a judge. If you have been relying on librarians or experts to tell you whether it's OK to use copyrighted material in a particular way, this approach may make you uncomfortable at first. When it comes to fair use, certainty is only achieved after a case has been brought before the courts, tried, and a judge has ruled. But as the reasoning process of fair use relies on the concept of good faith, in the absence of certainty, it's important to articulate your reasoning and be able to explain it to others.

Inspired by Harry Potter

The concept of *derivative work* has expanded greatly over the years, thanks to the interests of the global media industry. Authors' copyright is protected when related new works are created that are based substantially on a preexisting work. Derivative products include translations, musical arrangements, dramatizations, and movies based on books.

However, derivative works are not automatically considered a violation of copyright: Some may be licensed derivatives, others may be infringing, and still others may be protected under the doctrine of fair use.

When Warner Brothers and J. K. Rowling, author of the *Harry Potter* books, sued Steven Vander Ark, a librarian, it made the nightly news. Vander Ark created a reference book that organizes information from the voluminous Potter universe into an easy-to-use supplement. He did not seek a license or ask permission from Rowling to write his book. He's a fan who is a reference librarian: Over a period of several years, he created an authoritative reference to the fictional world of Harry Potter. Vander Ark's book did not add much in the way of commentary and analysis of wizards, Muggles, and such; instead, it cross-referenced the many obscure references and allusions in the series.

In a highly publicized decision issued on September 8, 2008, U.S. District Court Judge Robert Patterson ruled that Steven Vander Ark's *Harry Potter Lexicon* was a copyright infringement. But as American Library Association lawyer Jonathan Band writes, "Although J. K. Rowling prevailed in the litigation, the big winner actually was fair use."[13] Why?

Vander Ark's encyclopedia was ruled to be transformative even though it did not contain significant commentary or analysis. Providing "an alphabetized catalogue of elements from the Harry Potter world" was what made the book transformative. Even though Rowling herself claimed she was intending to someday write such a reference book herself, the judge ruled that she could not control the market for reference guides to the *Harry Potter* works, writing that "The market for reference guides does not become derivative simply because the copyright holder seeks to produce or license one."[14]

In the end, the judge sided with Rowling, believing that Vander Ark simply quoted *too much* of Rowling's work in composing the encyclopedia. Vander Ark's book did contain lengthy verbatim copies or close paraphrases of descriptions in the *Harry Potter* novels, along with information that Rowling had included in her own reference books about the Potter universe. This, the judge ruled, was taking more than was necessary. The judge could have awarded damages as high as $1.35 million, but instead assessed only the minimum amount, $6,750—perhaps reflecting a belief that Steven Vander Ark had a reasonable belief that his use of the *Harry Potter* works was a fair use.

Thank goodness that Steven Vander Ark was represented by the Fair Use Project of Stanford Law School's Center for Internet and Society. This and other legal clinics, housed at major law schools, help to level the playing field for creative people whose work depends on the use of copyrighted materials. Without them, the case might never have come before the court. But because of their support, there will likely be more latitude for creative works of this sort in the future.

The Issue of Market Impact

Educators know that the nature of composing requires the use of others' materials. But teachers should avoid making what Martine Courant Rife calls a "fair use *faux pas*" by requiring that students *always* ask permission.[15] Some teachers ask students to always seek permission when using images or require students to choose among Creative Commons or "copyright free" images in their designs.[16] Both of these actions send the wrong message about fair use, distorting and limiting students' ability to be creative. Such recommendations deny their legal rights under fair use.

When using others' work in our own academic and creative work, we should use only what is necessary to accomplish our goals and frankly self-assess whether we are simply copying or whether our use of the copy is part of a new work that is truly "our own." It's appropriate to answer these questions:

- How will my use of the materials affect the copyright owner's ability to profit from their work?
- Will my use of this work cause excessive economic harm to the copyright owner?

Notice that these questions do *not* include "Am I making money from the use of copyrighted material?"

Courts have clearly established that copyright owners are not entitled to an absolute monopoly over transformative uses of their works. As the Dorling Kindersley case showed, people can profit from their transformative use of other people's copyrighted materials because *new creative works create new audiences, new interpretations, and new markets.*

When someone's use of copyrighted materials *substitutes for, supplants, or replaces* the owner's core business market, however, it is likely to be a violation of copyright.

For example, a teacher who takes a lesson plan from another teacher's published book of lesson plans and puts it on her own Web site is probably violating copyright. Her work has the same purpose and the same audience as the original. However, it's probably not a copyright violation to link to materials that are freely available digitally, especially if your link makes clear the location of the original source. If your link makes it seem like the content is yours, however, that might be a problem.

When people copy simply to avoid creating something themselves or to avoid making a purchase, a mental red flag should be raised—that's likely to be a violation of copyright. Sadly, these practices are common among many in K–12 education. As we learned in Chapter 2, many teachers feel they are doing God's work and that copying to any degree in the service of education is permitted. This is neither legally nor morally defensible.

Making Copies for Whom? For What Purpose?

One of the reasons why educators are confused about copying is the prominence of "reproducibles"—these are K–12 materials created for student use. As educators know, the process of creating reproducibles takes creativity and imagination. There are ordinary, run-of-the-mill reproducibles, and then there are reproducibles worth paying for. A high-quality reproducible can be a powerful resource for teaching and learning. Sometimes, these tools can even support a teacher's own intellectual development, introducing them to new ideas and innovative approaches to pedagogy while supporting student learning at the same time.

When a teacher buys a book or multimedia resource that contains reproducibles, it is understood that he or she is entitled to make multiple copies, year after year, to use in the classroom with students.

But although it's lawful to make copies for student use, it's not lawful to copy a large portion of the book of reproducibles and share it with lots of other teachers. Why? In this case, the copies are not for classroom use. Instead, they reach the same audience for the same purpose as the original work. The copies are, in effect, a substitute for purchasing the book itself.

FIRST-SALE DOCTRINE

Once you own a legally acquired copy of a creative work, you have a lot of freedom to do what you want with it. You can rip it into strips and create a collage. You can throw it on a bonfire. You can put it up for sale on eBay. The Copyright Act of 1976 says that when you buy a legally produced copyrighted work, you can sell or loan that copy to others.

Libraries heavily depend on this doctrine to lend books and other items to patrons—so, like fair use, the first-sale doctrine is a user right.

The teacher who created the reproducible (and the publisher who brought the creative work to market) has the right to profit from her work. Of course, after we have purchased a copyrighted work, the *first-sale doctrine* gives us the right to sell or give away that work without asking permission. So, it's OK for us to share, sell, or give away our copy of the actual object—in this case, the wonderful lesson plans we find in a book we have bought. But it's not a fair use to make multiple copies of other people's books and distribute them just so someone else doesn't have to buy it themselves—that is an act that clearly deprives the author of revenue. Making multiple copies to share with lots of people may supplant or replace the owner's right to profit from his or her work, limiting legitimate sales for the book. That's not fair.

So, the concept of transformativeness helps us understand the social value of fair use as a means to promote creativity and the spread of knowledge. But we have also seen that there are examples of nontransformative copying, where the purpose is to avoid paying for the work and where there is no significant adding of value or repurposing.

PIRACY

Some people use file-sharing networks to upload and download software, music, movies, TV shows, games, and images. There's a great debate in our culture about these practices since the media industry opposes file sharing while, in general, the public supports it.

However, when people use peer-to-peer sharing simply to bypass the cost of legally acquiring a copy, this is likely to be a violation of copyright law.

But peer-to-peer technology itself is not illegal. While many of the materials available on peer-to-peer networks are not lawfully made copies, some are. It's also legal to use these networks to share materials that are specifically licensed for sharing or are in the public domain.

When Educators Violate Copyright: A Case Study

Joy Smithfield (a pseudonym) is an educator who wrote a book of lesson plans and activities that was published by a professional-education organization. The book retails for a little over $50 and is well regarded in the field, with glowing reviews from several professional-educational publications establishing it as a "must have" resource.

When she attended a state education conference, she arrived at the registration desk and was handed a binder of resource materials along with the conference schedule. Imagine her surprise when she opened up the binder and discovered page after page of her own materials—more than 1/3 of the total book, with identifying information from the pages removed!

Someone involved in organizing the conference did not consider the legal issues involved in reproducing large portions of a copyrighted work and offering it to large numbers of people without permission. They reproduced the copies for the same purpose and the same audience as Joy Smithfield was reaching with her book.

"What hurt most," explained Joy, "was that nobody even asked me." She felt completely disrespected by the conference organizers. "If I had been asked, I might have given permission to share it freely, even though the material is available for sale." Joy decided not to sue for copyright infringement, although she could have. Instead, she used it as a chance to inform her colleagues about copyright and fair use.

Be Reasonable: The Good-Faith Defense

I love this quote from Carrie Russell of the American Library Association: "Fair use cannot be reduced to a checklist. Fair use requires that people think."[17] But, since all people do not think alike, when educators make a fair-use determination, they might or might not be in line with what a court might eventually determine, should there be a lawsuit.

Fortunately, there is a provision of the law that considers whether the user acted reasonably and in good faith, in light of general practice in his or her particular field. If an employee of a nonprofit educational institution has made a rational and reasonable fair-use determination, he or she is not likely to be targeted for an infringement lawsuit because of Section 504(c)(2) of the Copyright Act of 1976, the *reasonableness standard*.

Under this provision of the law, a court must remit statutory damages to zero in any case where an infringer believed, and had reasonable grounds for believing, that his or her use of the copyrighted work was a fair use. This provision applies only if the infringer was an employee of a nonprofit educational institution, a library, or an archive and was acting within the scope of his or her employment.[18]

The good-faith defense is intended to protect educators who are doing their job well—and it's another reason why educators shouldn't be afraid to use their fair use rights.

Copyright Violation Threats, Real and Imagined

As we have seen in this chapter, fair use depends on a consideration of the totality of the individual circumstances. There can be no checklists or shortcuts: Context and situation determine how fair use applies. We may consider the author's original intent and the changes or creative contributions made, which may add value or repurpose a preexisting copyrighted work. We may consider the audiences and their interpretations of the new work, as it is similar to or different from the original. We recognize the importance of thinking broadly about whether the new work benefits society more than it hurts the copyright holder.

Now, you know *why* there is very little case law that can be used to nail down, once and for all, how the doctrine of fair use specifically applies to a particular K–12 educational situation. To the best of my knowledge, there has never been a lawsuit decided by a judge where a teacher has been sued for the educational use of copyrighted materials. This chapter has shown you why such cases do not exist. Neither have we found any evidence of a lawsuit where a student was charged with copyright violation for the use of copyrighted work within academic or creative work produced as part of a class assignment. A copyright holder would be foolish to bring such a lawsuit because the 1976 Copyright Act broadly enables the use of copyrighted materials for educational purposes.

It's not fair to make large numbers of copies and distribute them in ways that replace or substitute for the original work. But that's different from making a limited number of copies of material that you're using for teaching and learning—this is permitted under fair use.

As we learned in Chapter 2, if you distribute creative work that has copyrighted content embedded in it, it's possible that a media company will try using a cease-and-desist letter as a scare tactic. These letters first warn the user that a particular use of copyrighted materials may be a violation and then request that material be removed. Some people believe that getting a letter means that they will be sued. This is inaccurate. There are many steps between the writing of a letter and the filing of a lawsuit. Cease-and-desist letters are easy and cheap, and often they are sent because they are effective— they create fear. We suspect that many of the vague stories we have heard about copyright in education come, not from a lawsuit, but from a letter.

Students may have experienced "takedowns" on their Facebook, MySpace, or other Web sites. Copyrighted music, print materials, and video can be removed from YouTube and other social networking Web sites under a specific provision of the Digital Millennium Copyright Act (DMCA). As Wendy Seltzer, professor at American University and founder of Chilling Effects.org, points out, the moment a copyright holder claims an infringement, the law encourages the middleman (in this case YouTube, the service provider) to remove the offending material. The service provider takes down content—even in situations where there is a legitimate fair use— rather than face even a remote chance of liability. Until the DMCA is revised appropriately or exemptions are available for those who want to make fair use of encrypted material, this law will limit people's ability to create and distribute materials that involve appropriation, remixing and sampling for educational purposes.[19]

Fair use is the part of copyright law that enables and supports human creativity. Artists and creative people will inevitably use

YOUTUBE TAKEDOWNS

A teenager sings "Winter Wonderland" and posts it to YouTube. One day, the video mysteriously disappears from the Web site because the song is owned by Warner Music. The teen, believing her use to be a fair use, immediately posts another YouTube video to document the takedown experience.

As part of the Digital Millennium Copyright Act of 1998 (DMCA), Congress granted online service providers (companies like Facebook and YouTube) certain protections from copyright infringement liability. To get this protection, they must implement a **notice-and-takedown system**, removing content within a specific time period if a copyright holder complains.

Digital watermarks can be used to identify when YouTube videos have included excerpts of copyrighted works. But these tools *cannot* distinguish between a fair use of copyrighted material and an infringement. And while YouTube offers users the option to dispute a removal or send a formal DMCA **counternotice**, many YouTube users, lacking legal help, are afraid to take action. Fortunately, a number of university legal clinics that specialize in intellectual property law offer free legal services to help in such cases.

the products of contemporary culture in making art. That's why the Los Angeles–based street artist Shepard Fairey has sued the Associated Press (AP), which has been threatening him with a copyright-infringement suit. The poster artist is asking a judge to clarify that his use of an AP photograph (as inspiration in creating the famous Obama "Hope" poster) is protected under the doctrine of fair use.[20] A ruling on this decision will influence artists and creative individuals around the country.

According to legal scholar Michael Madison, critics from the art world say that Fairey's whole career has emphasized the appropriation of historical images, often images with salient and significant political force.[21] Appropriation art is a genre that is widely recognized in the art world. But citizens can (and should) make their own analysis of fair use claims. The fair use doctrine has flexibility that allows it to accommodate changes in technology, as well as changes in educational practice.

Students strengthen their media literacy by combining symbolic forms such as language, images, sound, and digital media to express and share meaning.

4

Fair Use and Digital Learning

Social studies teacher Spiro Bolos was trying to help students understand the global economic crisis of 2009. What were the connections between the bankers and investors on Wall Street and the many people who were losing their homes in the subprime financial meltdown? It's not easy to get students—or anyone else—to understand the $70 trillion global banking industry and its role in the recent economic recession.

Listening to a segment on the issue from *This American Life* on National Public Radio (NPR) on his way home from work one day, Mr. Bolos wanted to find a way to motivate students to learn more about global economics. Perhaps students could listen carefully to the NPR broadcast, understand the ideas, and make connections to the social studies curriculum. But what would make that activity engaging and personally meaningful for high school students?

He came up with an idea: Students could create multimedia visuals to illustrate the various key ideas presented in the broadcast. To make effective slides, they would have to listen carefully to the broadcast to understand the ideas and then develop a creative way to visually represent part of the information using images, language, and graphic design. Their goal was to create slides that would be appropriate and effective in communicating ideas to their peers.

Each student was responsible for one short segment of the one-hour broadcast. For example, as one banker described "no income verification" loans, he described the bank's loan approval process, saying, "We're setting you up to lie." To illustrate this point, the high school student chose an image of Pinocchio, with his nose growing long, looking sheepish. Figure 4.1 shows an image, created by a student to illustrate a point in the broadcast concerning high-risk loans, loans "so high risk they're toxic." As part of the assignment, Mr. Bolos asked students to use attribution by indicating the source of the images they used in their work.

Mr. Bolos considered this assignment a success: Students did learn a lot about the roots of the global financial crisis. Each student brainstormed a way to visualize an idea and then gathered additional resources on the topic. To prepare a slide, they had to

Figure 4.1   Student-Created Slide From the Financial Meltdown Project

deploy principles of effective graphic design. Media literacy education came in as students considered the unique communicative potential of visual images and verbal language in creating their messages.

When Mr. Bolos screened the broadcast with the students' own slides attached, there was attentive listening and a lot of pride evident in the classroom as students acknowledged the creative work of their peers in visualizing complex concepts in banking and economics. In the debriefing session, Mr. Bolos encouraged students to explain how their visuals added value and created new meanings for the broadcast. He could see immediately that students were proud of what they had learned about the financial crisis—many students told him that, since the project was completed, they were able to explain the details of the economic crisis to peers, parents, and family members.

Mr. Bolos' assignment made substantial use of an entire 60-minute segment from *This American Life*—a copyrighted work. However, the context and use of this work was new—students added value to the audio broadcast with the use of visuals they created themselves. Not only did the visuals demonstrate their comprehension skills, they made the broadcast more informative and engaging for other high school students. Still, he wondered if he should share the assignment at a national conference. Should he post the assignment on his blog?

Are Educators Up for the Challenge?

After a lifetime living with those charts and graphs that define educational use guidelines as 10% or 30 seconds of a song or no more than 2,000 words of an article, Mr. Bolos knew that this particular assignment would not fit with those old ways of conceptualizing fair use. Right now, in the field of education, what we've gotten out of those charts and graphs is copyright confusion, which interferes with innovative uses of technologies in education.

Fortunately for his students, Mr. Bolos also knew that he had the right to make a fair-use determination. He knew that the doctrine of fair use adapts to changing times, changing technologies, and—perhaps most importantly—changing approaches to teaching and learning. After reviewing the *Code of Best Practices for Media Literacy Education*[1] and considering the context and situation, he decided to post the student-created slides—with the NPR broadcast—online.

We've seen, in Chapter 3, that while the doctrine of fair use is designed to support the educational use of copyrighted material, it requires critical thinking and analysis skills to make a fair-use determination because not every use of copyrighted material in education is a fair use.

You're probably wondering if teachers and students will be up for the challenge.

I believe they are, but it's a challenge that teachers can't manage alone—we need support from our community of colleagues and peers. That's why it's important for educators, as a community of practitioners, to develop a consensus on how the doctrine of fair use applies to our work. We also need to get comfortable in making a fair-use determination.

In this chapter, I describe the process used to develop a *Code of Best Practices in Fair Use for Media Literacy Education*, a document that articulates this consensus and increases teachers' comfort level with applying the doctrine of fair use. After we understand this document and its importance, we'll take a look at teaching about copyright and fair use in K–12 educational settings. After all, when you teach something, that's when you really learn it well.

Communities of Practice Define Fair Use

Exercising your rights makes them stronger. That's what people have discovered over the more than 230-year history of American democracy. The doctrine of fair use is an inherent part of copyright law—it enables society to benefit both from the copyright holder's ability to exploit his or her work in the marketplace and from the user's ability to use the copyrighted work without payment or permission under some circumstances.

The doctrine of fair use is a user right and it has to be understood in the context of existing patterns and practices of how particular groups of people make creative use of copyrighted work.[2] These patterns will vary for many reasons. Art historians will make use of copyrighted materials in ways that are different from the work of documentary filmmakers, who will use materials differently from those in education, in software development, in medicine, or in the arts.

The practice of education changes over time. Certainly, educators in 1912 used copyrighted materials in their work with students in differently than contemporary educators. Over time, people will use copyrighted works in different ways because technologies and teaching methods change to meet the needs of students and society.

WHAT HAPPENED TO *EYES ON THE PRIZE?*

Eyes on the Prize[3] is a film series that disappeared. Well, not literally. But copyright restrictions have dramatically limited its availability. *Eyes on the Prize* is an award-winning 14-part documentary series, created in 1987, that chronicles the American civil rights movement. It is considered the most comprehensive documentary series ever produced, showing the inspiring leadership of Martin Luther King and ordinary citizens like Rosa Parks, who refused to give up her seat to a white man on a bus in Montgomery, Alabama. The film weaves together film clips from 82 archives, 287 still photos, and 120 song titles, along with interviews from civil rights movement participants recalling their experiences.

At the time when the producer, Henry Hampton, negotiated license fees for the first national broadcast on PBS, he was an unknown independent producer. He purchased licenses for a 10-year period. But after the series won more than 20 national awards, and after Henry Hampton died, the business of relicensing the clips fell to his heirs. With expired licenses, the series could not be broadcast, and it could not be reproduced or sold. At one time, the Ford Foundation estimated that the license renewal process would cost $5 million.

Why so expensive? Big music companies, like EMI, would not offer reasonable rates for the music used in the series. The use of specific songs, like the scene where a group of people sing "Happy Birthday to You" to Martin Luther King, was a particular problem. Warner Chappell owns the copyright to the "Happy Birthday" song, which earns $2 million annually in license fees. Because the Copyright Term Extension Act of 1998 added additional years of protection, the "Happy Birthday" song will not enter the public domain until the year 2030.[4]

Fortunately, there is a bit of good news. A grass-roots campaign developed to rescue the film. The Ford Foundation provided nearly $1 million to enable some episodes of the series to be broadcast on PBS in February 2008, nearly 20 years after its original premiere.[5] But, this case really illustrates the point that without fair use, copyright can become an instrument of private censorship, limiting the public's access to information and ideas.

User communities can establish for themselves a reasoned, self-reflective, and normative understanding of how fair use applies to their social and creative practices. They can expect this consensus to be respected by other decision makers, including the courts.

One Community: Documentary Filmmakers

One such user community—creative people who make active use of copyrighted materials—is documentary filmmakers. They often need to quote from the visual materials owned by others in order to make their own work. However, as a result of the high costs and complicated process of paying license fees or getting permission (clearing rights) to use copyrighted images, texts, or sounds in their work, some documentary filmmakers avoided making films that addressed certain topics. They also changed sound, images and locations in their films in order to avoid copyright problems.[6]

Like educators, documentary filmmakers suffered from an overly strict interpretation of intellectual property and copyright law. They were not taking advantage of their rights to claim fair use. It was affecting the quality of the work they produced.

Patricia Aufderheide and Peter Jaszi met with documentary filmmakers in small groups to help them assert their legal rights. Under the philosophy that creative communities need to come to their own clearly articulated consensus (or best practices) about what is fair and reasonable under the law, they created the *Documentary Filmmakers' Statement of Best Practices in Fair Use.*[7] It identifies four common practices that documentary filmmakers need to do as part of their own creative work. Documentary filmmakers can:

- use copyrighted materials as the object of social, political, or cultural critique;
- quote copyrighted works of popular culture to illustrate an argument or point;
- capture copyrighted media content in the process of filming something else; and
- use copyrighted material in a historical sequence.

Since its publication, the statement has proved to be an educational tool for the documentary-filmmaker community. For example, Byron Hurt's powerful media literacy film, *Beyond Beats and Rhymes*[8] was successfully released on PBS in 2006. In this film, Hurt uses clips of music videos to comment on the misogynistic messages about gender, race, and power in the work of popular rap musicians. Without the *Statement of Best Practices*, that film might never have been made.

Creating a Code of Best Practices for Educators

Building on the work of Jaszi and Aufderheide with documentary filmmakers, we set about to construct a similar statement for educators. We focused on those who self-identify as media literacy educators. Not only do they work at all levels and disciplines but they also make active use of copyrighted materials from mass media, popular culture, and digital technologies to strengthen students' critical thinking and communication skills.

First, we conducted individual interviews with 60 K–12 teachers, college and university teachers, and those working in youth media organizations. From these interviews, we created a series of hypothetical scenarios that reflected the most frequently mentioned challenges, questions, or concerns about how copyright applied to their work. Nearly 150 individuals participated from U.S. cities including New York, San Francisco, Philadelphia, Chicago, Boston, and other cities.

Each group was first introduced to the general principles of copyright and fair use and then invited to consider hypothetical scenarios pertaining to the use of copyrighted materials for (1) classroom instruction, (2) curriculum development, and (3) student multimedia production. In exploring these hypothetical scenarios, participants brought their own experiences to bear on analyzing the hypothetical cases.

In the beginning, teachers lacked confidence to make reasoned judgments themselves. Some kept looking to an expert (a lawyer or academic) to tell them the "right" answer. Sometimes, library media specialists positioned themselves (or were positioned) as enforcers of copyright policy. We educators are accustomed to relying on others for expertise on this topic.

In many schools, school administrators—sometimes as a result of fear, ignorance, or laziness—take an ultraconservative view on copyright, urging teachers to err on the safe side. Just don't use copyrighted materials at all, some have been told. Stick to the stuff the district has bought. Don't bring in anything extra.

But no teacher feels comfortable with that—because we are dedicated to meeting the needs of our students. We naturally seek out resources and materials to meet our learning objectives. We want our students to engage with their culture—their cultural heritage, past and present—to develop critical reasoning and communication skills. This will almost inevitably involve the use of copyrighted materials.

As teachers started to tease out the nuances of the hypothetical scenarios, you could see the light bulbs going on. They recognized that there are several common instructional practices where the use of copyrighted materials is simply normative, part of what is essential for the practice of teaching and learning. Figure 4.2 shows the consensus that emerged from these discussions. These are the central tenents of the *Code of Best Practices in Fair use for Media Literacy Education*.[9]

Figure 4.2   The Code of Best Practices in Fair Use for Media Literacy Education

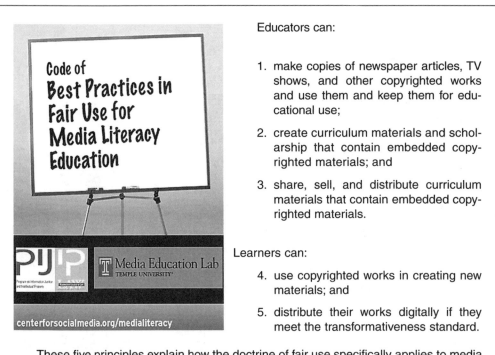

Educators can:

1. make copies of newspaper articles, TV shows, and other copyrighted works and use them and keep them for educational use;

2. create curriculum materials and scholarship that contain embedded copyrighted materials; and

3. share, sell, and distribute curriculum materials that contain embedded copyrighted materials.

Learners can:

4. use copyrighted works in creating new materials; and

5. distribute their works digitally if they meet the transformativeness standard.

These five principles explain how the doctrine of fair use specifically applies to media literacy education, but the principles are also useful in relation to a wide range of educational uses of media and technology for teaching and learning.

Compare and Contrast: Strengthening Fair-Use Reasoning

To illustrate the fair-use reasoning process, we asked educators to compare and contrast two different (fictional) educators in the same school whose students were making use of copyrighted materials. We based these scenarios on the real-world stories offered to us by educators we had interviewed.

Consider Mrs. Alhumaidan's and Mrs. Johnson's students, whose class activities are described in the boxes that follow. In each scenario, the copyright question is

> *Can student-created slides containing digitized, copyrighted still images be uploaded so parents can view children's work?*

In the process of discussing whether Mrs. Alhumaidan's students needed to ask permission to use copyrighted images in their projects,

IMOVIE PROJECT ABOUT STEREOTYPES IN THE MEDIA

After reading *Holes* by Louis Sacher, Mrs. Alhumaidan has assigned students to create an iMovie video about stereotypes of teenagers in the media. She wanted students to reflect more deeply on how stereotypes work in fiction and wanted to explore the representation of adolescence in the mass media.

Students used spoken-word poetry with various copyrighted still images featuring characters from TV shows and movies and images of teen celebrities found in magazines and online. Mrs. Alhumaidan wanted to post the videos online so that parents could be encouraged to discuss the topic of stereotypes with their children.

If the use of copyrighted materials is not a fair use, then teachers and students can ask permission, pay a license fee, or use copyright-cleared materials that have been granted a Creative Commons license. What action is fair and reasonable?

some key ideas emerged. Should this type of project be shared on the school's Web site, so teachers could encourage students to share discussions about stereotypes with their parents as a means of extending student learning? Would it be fair to share some samples of students' work for other purposes, like sharing ideas about technology integration with other educators?

In our focus groups, we discovered that educators needed to use the concepts of author, purpose, and audience to make a reasoned claim for (or against) fair use. The first step is to determine whether the doctrine of fair use applies to the particular use of a copyrighted work.

When discussing the "stereotypes in the media" project, most teachers in our focus groups believed that the work's essential purpose, as a work of critical commentary, clearly entitled it to the protection of fair use. The work could be displayed publicly on the school's Web site. When a particular use of copyrighted materials is determined to be a fair use, permission from the copyright holder is not required. And the material can be shared for many purposes: to promote parent–child communication, to share with educators, as a tool for social advocacy, or even to make money.

> ## SLIDE PRESENTATION ON COUNTRIES OF THE WORLD
>
> Mrs. Johnson worked with her technology specialist to create an activity for her elementary students. Students created PowerPoint slides using copyrighted images they gathered through Google to illustrate their reports on countries of the world. Each student selected a country to explore and gathered information about various cultural traditions, including the names of major cities, cultural landmarks, geography, family life, and food. Students gathered information about the country and composed a slide presentation that combines images and language.
>
> Mrs. Johnson wants to upload their completed slides to the school's public Web site so that parents could see their children's creative work. What action is fair and reasonable?

When asked to consider the similarities and differences between the Mrs. Alhumaidan's and Mrs. Johnson's activities, many teachers in our focus groups viewed both activities as a form of media literacy education where the fair use of copyrighted materials was appropriate and justified. Why?

- Students strengthen media literacy skills in both activities by creating messages and using symbolic forms such as language, images, sound, and digital media to express and share meaning.
- In learning to select appropriate still images or video excerpts, students learn how the juxtaposition and sequencing of images shapes meaning. In their use of presentation software or video editing tools, they discover how the technology tool itself shapes the kind of messages that can be created.

A few teachers, however, saw things differently. Because the doctrine of fair use involves reasoning and critical analysis, people will sometimes make different determinations. Some teachers believed that the doctrine of fair use only protects Mrs. Alhumaidan's student-produced work in critically analyzing media's stereotypes of teens and does not protect Mrs. Johnson's students who select images to illustrate their learning of geography. Some teachers focus on the language of Section 107 of the copyright law—the part that specifically states that "comment and criticism" are examples of fair use.

But this does not mean that *only* works that have as their purpose commentary and criticism are entitled to the fair-use provision. The examples provided in the statute ("purposes such as criticism, comment, news reporting, teaching, scholarship or research") are just that—examples.

As we saw in Chapter 3, many different types of educational uses of copyrighted materials are clearly fair use; and some educational uses of copyrighted material are clearly an infringement, as in the case of the educator who reproduced the reproducibles to share with other teachers or the conference administrator who copied a third of a book to share with 300 of her colleagues.

That's why educators need to use reasoning and judgment, considering the specific situation and asking about the larger social balance that is at the heart of fair-use reasoning: Does the specific use of copyrighted works benefit society more than it hurts the copyright holder?

STEPS IN THE REASONING PROCESS

1. Determine if the doctrine of fair use applies to your particular use of a copyrighted work.

2. If so, use the copyrighted work freely in your own creative work.

3. If not, then ask permission of the copyright holder.

4. Pay a license fee if needed.

5. Or use copyright cleared resources (like Creative Commons) as an alternative selection.

What About Permissions?

When the use of copyrighted materials by educators or students doesn't fall within the doctrine of fair use, it's necessary to seek permission. This process can occasionally be easy—as when we e-mail a photographer about a Flickr photo that we want to use as an illustration for a book cover—or it can be challenging, as in the process of figuring out who at Time Warner to contact—about anything.

We've already learned about the many circumstances when permissions are not required, and we have reviewed the advantages and disadvantages of licensing. The process of seeking permissions for student media productions is one of those topics where teachers have different views, each deserving respect. When the minimum fee for the use of a single pop song is $288, many teachers will reject the concept of permission seeking as completely inappropriate for students who are, say, enrolled in an introduction to video production elective.

However, depending on their background and professional orientation, other teachers see asking permission as an ethical, if not always legal, matter. It's a courtesy, some teachers tell us. You should ask permission because "it's the right thing to do."

But, other teachers point out that when we write an essay about the supernatural imagination and quote a passage from the book *Angel Time*, we don't feel any ethical obligation to e-mail or call Anne Rice to ask permission. So, teachers' ideas about permissions will naturally reflect their professional backgrounds, ethical values, and life experiences.

Some teachers believe it's important for students to learn the practices used by professionals in media industries. For instance, some teachers who teach in professional schools (colleges that are training people to work in the industry) require students to use the *Documentary Filmmakers' Statement of Best Practices in Fair Use*[10] to make a determination of fair use. This perspective is also common among those high school teachers who have formerly worked in broadcasting or corporate media industries. As we have seen, each professional community of practitioners determines the norms and expectations about the use of copyrighted materials in the context of their work.

Yet, as in any community, there may be nuances within the ranks. For example, a producer making a corporate documentary for Monsanto about the wonders of genetically engineered tomatoes that uses a clip owned by the Discovery Channel may feel obliged to buy a license in the interest of protecting the transnational corporation from potential liability. But an independent producer who is reporting on genetically engineered foods and illustrates her documentary with the same clip may comfortably claim fair use and not feel the need to ask permission of the giant firm. Both approaches make sense because these different situations relate to the larger political and economic context of the use.

Sadly, in many educational institutions, there is a culture of ignorance and fear that contributes to a tendency to believe that permissions are *always* required when using a copyrighted work. In my work with teachers, I found that because many educators had themselves used copyrighted materials without permission, they sometimes had a misplaced feeling of guilt, leading them to either be silent about both fair use and permissions or to encourage hypercompliance.

Permission seeking is appropriate when students are not making transformative use of copyrighted materials, as when popular music is used in a video simply as background music, to set a mood, or to attract attention due to its familiarity, appeal or popularity. But each case needs to be considered on its own merits. In some cases, the use of music serves the same value and purpose that it was originally designed for. For example, when students create music videos, their use of copyrighted music can supplant, replace, or serve as a substitute for the original. Seeking permission is appropriate. However, in other cases, the combination of music and images repurposes the music in a way that is truly transformative.

PAYING FOR CONTENT WITH A LICENSE

Licensing is a term for the process of paying a fee to the copyright owner for your use of the work. When you ask permission, you describe the work, your planned use of it, and the audience for the work. In some cases, there is a permissions-management company that serves as a middleman who establishes fees and collects revenue on behalf of the owner. Some schools offer teachers and students licensed access to copyrighted material through databases or video-streaming services.

There are some conveniences to these systems and some disadvantages. The biggest downside: If you access copyrighted material using a licensing system, you cannot claim fair use. You must abide by the terms of the contract, which may have terms that are more restrictive than what copyright law mandates. The terms of these contracts can be densely written and complicated to understand.

A license may state that any copying of student handouts must be unaltered—educators cannot edit, crop, resize, or colorize them. And although some video streaming services do allow students to select bits for use in their own work, they generally do not permit this work to be displayed outside of the classroom setting. In this case, students who use a video excerpt in a class project could not make even a single copy of their class project to take home and show to their parents. By contrast, a student who accessed the video independently, without a licensing system, could claim fair use.

We shouldn't let license agreements diminish our legal rights. A good license is one that protects the rights of both copyright owners and users. Look for a statement like this: "Nothing in this License shall in any way exclude, modify, or affect any of Licensee's statutory or common law rights under the copyright laws of the United States."

When the use of copyrighted materials merely retransmits the material in nontransformative ways that interfere with the market for the original, educators should model the permissions process. This will help students to distinguish between material that should be licensed, material that is in the public domain or otherwise openly available, and copyrighted material that is subject to fair use.

Attribution: Giving Credit Where Credit Is Due

Educators hate plagiarism—using the work of another without giving credit or cutting and pasting someone else's material into your own work. We value attribution, something we generally call "citing your sources." But teachers are misinforming students when they say that any use of any copyrighted material is OK as long as you cite the source. This is a common misunderstanding that deserves correction. You can cite your sources and still violate copyright. That's why it's important to separate the concepts and consider them distinctly.

Library media specialists want to see attribution in every single example of student-produced work. This is a well-meaning effort but sometimes can be inappropriately rigid. It's true that some teachers do a poor job of teaching the appropriate forms of citation. But most teachers use their judgment in determining when and how to have students use attribution. Educators must be free to determine when and how to require attribution in student productions, based on judgments about the developmental level of the learner and the purpose of the assignment. Sometimes, teachers will require attribution in student creative and academic work, but not in all cases.

For example, when students create a video public-service announcement (PSA) in science class to encourage others to recycle, it's not appropriate for them to include a list of credits at the end of their PSA, indicating the source of the facts stated in the voiceover. Why? The form of the PSA does not call for attribution. The PSA needs to end with a call to action, not a citation list. Each form and genre of expression has different conventions regarding attribution.

Some educators emphasize the need to establish rigid rules proscribing attribution for *each and every* use of copyrighted work in student media productions. But others point out that, for most of the 20th century, students could sometimes demonstrate their knowledge by creating a print poster board with text and images cut out from magazines and newspapers. Would an educator be expected to use attribution for *every* such assignment? How onerous and developmentally inappropriate to require young children to write detailed citation lists for this type of assignment!

Teachers know that teaching about attribution is important. But we need to be able to use our judgment and reasoning to determine when and how attribution fits into our overall instructional goals. For example, in the PSA assignment, a high school science teacher can require students to submit a list of key resources, presented as a print document, enabling students to identify the resources they used in exploring the topic of recycling. But an elementary school teacher might only involve students in a discussion about the different types of resources they used to gather information: books, Web sites, and newspaper articles.

We can't neglect attention to teaching about appropriate forms of attribution in the mistaken idea that some other teacher will cover it. Basic concepts of attribution are rooted in respect for authorship and reflect the necessity of borrowing and sharing as a part of the transmission of cultural and intellectual heritage.

Teaching About Copyright and Fair Use

In Resource A, at the back of this book, you'll find a detailed outline that will help you offer a staff-development program on copyright and fair use. When teachers discover how much fun it is to teach about copyright and fair use, they're often surprised.

But many educators—even school librarians—shy away from teaching about copyright. Not only are there numerous materials out there of questionable quality, as we saw in Chapter 2, but teachers often feel that they have to be "experts" on a topic.

However, growing up with an ever-growing array of devices for sharing, students understand quite well that communications and information technologies are shifting our conceptualization of copyright.

They know that teachers are not experts on the topics of copyright. But they're hungry to understand what the fuss is about when it comes to the issue. They love discussing the balance that's needed to protect both the rights of owners and users. That's why, with my own students, I begin an exploration of the topic of copyright with a *Schoolhouse Rock*–style music video, "What's Copyright?" In this video, a little animated bird lands on the windowsill of a big building in urban America, where he begins to sing,

Copyright's for the people.
Copyright is to promote creativity,
Balancing rights of owners and users of intellectual property.

But a character named Big C, high up in one of skyscrapers, argues with the little bird, singing,

I'm an owner, not a donor, copyright's for me.
Let me tell you how it's gonna be:
I'm the one who knows.

Look at all the things I own,
All the copyrights I hold,
All under my control.
Copyright's for the folks who own.[11]

We created this music video to help learners understand the purpose of copyright in the context of 21st-century culture, where

Users have rights too,
To critique, comment, and review.
First Amendment gives the right to use
Copyrighted works made by whoever.

As the animated bird inspires various musicians, video producers, and other artists, we hear from creative people on the streets, one of which points out

I'm a user, and I'm making my own
Inspired by the things I hear and see.
Face it, Big C:
Your fans are producers,
Your artists are users,
So balance is key.

Working collaboratively in partnership with Michael RobbGrieco and Geoff Beatty, we designed music videos that offer new information to students about the purpose of copyright and the definition of fair use as it applies especially to student media productions.

The lesson itself begins by activating students' prior knowledge about copyright. What do they already know? After viewing and listening to the music video, students write down the new ideas and information that was provided in the music video. With a partner, they identify additional questions they have now about the topic of copyright and fair use.

After viewing another music video titled, "Users' Rights, Section 107," students work with a partner to discuss some examples of creative works that rely on the concept of transformativeness. Students share their experiences of how transformativeness is found in television programs, movies, on YouTube, in music, and in the fine and popular arts.

SONG LYRICS FOR TEACHING ABOUT COPYRIGHT AND FAIR USE

Watch the music video at http://mediaeducationlab.com/2-user-rights-section-107-music-video.

Users' Rights, Section 107

User's rights! Section 107,
Of the Copyright Act of 1976,
The Doctrine of Fair Use tells us that we can
Use or quote stuff with no pay nor permission.

CHORUS

We can use or quote copyrighted material

Without permission or paying a license fee

When the cost to the copyright holder

Is less than the benefits for society.

Fair use has many strengths.

Most of all, it is flexible!

But some people find it too vague

Because it is contextual!

Context and situation

Determine how fair use applies.

Context and situation

Determine how fair use applies.

CHORUS

We can use or quote copyrighted material
Without permission or paying a license fee
When the cost to the copyright holder
Is less than the benefits for society.

BRIDGE

How will I know when fair use
Applies to my situation?
You must think of these four factors:
The nature of the use,

The purpose of the use,
The amount of the use,
And the effect on potential markets.
But there's really one really important factor:
Transformativeness, Transformativeness,
Transformativeness.
Add value! Repurpose!
Transformativeness.
Add value! Repurpose!
Transformativeness.
Add value! Repurpose!
Transformativeness.
Add value! Repurpose!

CHORUS

We can use or quote copyrighted material
Without permission or paying a license fee
When the cost to the copyright holder
Is less than the benefits for society.

BREAKDOWN

So, when you quote or use a copyrighted work,
Just ask yourself, "Did I repurpose?"
"Did I add value?"
"Did I repurpose?"
Ask myself "Why did I use it?"
Is it different from why it was created?
If it was, it's probably fair use
Did I add value
To the original in terms of the cultural
Or the money market value?
If I did, then it is fair use!

CHORUS

We can use or quote copyrighted material
Without permission or paying a license fee
When the cost to the copyright holder
Is less than the benefits for society.[13]

I also play one of the preview clips from the Media Education Foundation's videos, such as: *Tough Guise,* a film about how masculinity is represented in media, or *Deadly Persuasion,* about the marketing of alcohol and tobacco.[14] We discuss what types of copyrighted materials are used in the film. Are these uses of copyrighted work transformative?

Students can also be asked to generate examples of uses of a copyrighted work that are not transformative. Different people may employ different criteria in making a judgment about the meaning of the concepts of "repurpose" and "add value." Fair use is a concept that requires interpretation, and reasonable people will sometimes disagree about what constitutes a fair use. The goal is to use reasoning and evidence in making an interpretation.

Using Copyrighted Work to Make Something New

Using the concepts of *author, audience, purpose, point of view, context, subtext, message, format,* and *genre,* it's possible to open up important conversations about copyright and fair use with young people. For example, after learning about copyright and fair use, I ask students to select two YouTube videos and compose a comparison–contrast essay. One example should be a video that actively transforms copyrighted materials; the other choice should be a video that does not make transformative use. Students find it easy to find and locate these different types of uses— they're common on YouTube, My Space, and Facebook. In the essay, students describe each video and justify their selections, using reasoning to apply what they have learned about copyright and fair use.

Another assignment can explore the concept of "appropriation art," which is a fascinating topic to explore in the context of copyright and fair use. This genre of art explicitly involves the borrowing of other elements. In some cases, appropriation art has been identified as violating copyright. In other cases, it has been judged to be a fair use.[15]

Created by *Wall Street Journal* graphic designer David Klein, Figure 4.3[16] was designed to accompany an article in the newspaper. We see the subject of the cartoon torn with guilt about whether she is transforming or just copying. But savvy readers will be aware that the graphic designer himself is modifying and adapting the work of another artist, Roy Lichtenstein, who became famous in the art world for his copies of comic book panels.

Copyright controversies concerning artists including Andy Warhol and Jeff Koons can be used to understand more about the gray areas between transformative and derivative works.[17] It seems that art, in particular, is always building upon, modifying, and reworking other art.

 Figure 4.3 Appropriation Art: Readers Make the Connection to Identify the Source Materials Used

Source: David Klein

By activating critical thinking, teachers can help students recognize and make distinctions between illegal pirating and legal fair use.

5

The Future of Copyright

Lots of teachers use movie clips as part of classroom teaching. Science teachers use videos about cell mitosis and plate tectonics to help students visualize the small and large processes at work in biology and geology. English language arts teachers routinely use films based on literature—sometimes in ways that build literacy, critical thinking and analysis skills, and sometimes as a way to appreciate the artistry of film. Foreign-language teachers use foreign-language films to support listening comprehension. Elementary teachers use films to take students on "virtual field trips." And, history teachers are notorious for their use of historical D-day footage or dramatizations like *Glory* or *The Patriot*—sometimes using these works skillfully in ways that deepen student learning, and other times using these works merely to grab student attention, supplying a form of entertainment or a break from learning.

I don't use movies in my teaching very much anymore. Ten years ago, I used to examine the representation of newspaper editors using excerpts from *All the President's Men, Absence of Malice,* and *The Paper.* I used to show film clips in an academic-conference presentation to illustrate certain nuances of pedagogy and instruction concerning the use of film in education. But these days, in the classroom, DVDs are just plain cumbersome when it comes to effective use of film in the classroom.

Many teachers are in the same boat. When you're seeking to compare and contrast two versions of the balcony scene in different film adaptations of *Romeo and Juliet,* fast forwarding through trailers of *Hellboy, American Gangster,* and *Baby Mama* really spoils the mood. And because of the time it takes to load a DVD, the process is so time consuming that by the time you get the second scene cued up, the bell has rung and the period is over. So much for compare and contrast.

In the final chapter of this book, I share my experience in advocating for a change in the law that would permit educators to use film more effectively as a tool for media literacy education. Then, I share three visions of the future of copyright, unpacking some of the assumptions of each perspective in light of the needs of teachers and students.

Unlocking the Power of Film in Education

What teachers want and need, if they are to use film properly in the classroom, is to be able to create a set of digital clips that feature just the parts of the movie they want to use. But that common teaching practice has not been legal since 1998, when the Digital Millennium Copyright Act (DMCA) became law, making it illegal to bypass the Content Scrambling System (CSS) technology used in DVDs. The CSS technology makes it impossible to copy an excerpt. It's part of a highly controversial system of control used by media companies called *digital rights management.*

However, it is legal for people to create and use film-clip compilations. As we have learned in this book, under the doctrine of fair use, people can make noninfringing use of copyrighted materials for educational purposes. But at the present time, the DMCA law limits teachers' legal rights when it comes to certain forms of digital media.

That's why I found myself testifying before the U.S. Copyright Office on May 6, 2009, on behalf of K–12 teachers and students, asking them to unlock the power of film for education.[1] Along with film professors, representatives of the American Library Association, and other university library groups, I have asked the Copyright Office to issue a special exemption that would enable teachers and students to circumvent CSS technology to make clip compilations for educational use.

What Is Digital Rights Management (DRM) and Why Is It Controversial?

Digital rights management (DRM) is antipiracy technology used by some copyright owners to control who gets to access and copy their work. Software companies, movie, and music companies use

DRM to control how people install, listen to, view, and duplicate digital files. In whatever form it takes, DRM is, in essence, a digital padlock, protecting intellectual property from unauthorized copying. If you have ever had to use a special code to open, use, or copy a file, you've experienced DRM.

Critics say that DRM technologies do not stop copyright pirates, as evident from the vast quantity of illegal movie and music files available online. But DRM does interfere with fans' lawful use of music, movies, and other copyrighted works. People can't make a backup copy of a DVD they have purchased or use the portable media player of their choice.

The media industries say that DRM is an essential component of their business model. Without it, they say, the market for movies will evaporate, and they'll go out of business. But the Electronic Frontier Foundation states,

> Hollywood and the music industry have always attacked new technologies that help you get more from your media—these industries brought lawsuits against the VCR, DAT recorder, the MP3 player, and the PVR. Today, these media giants want to use DRM to take away your legitimate fair use and home recording rights, hoping to sell those rights back to you later. Worse still, recent DRM has invaded users' privacy and created severe security vulnerabilities in computers.[2]

How the DMCA Law Affects the Use of DVDs for Teaching and Learning

When the 1998 DMCA law made digital-rights management legal in ways that prevented educators from making fair use of copyrighted digital materials on DVDs, it also created a "safety valve" that empowered the Register of Copyright to authorize special exemptions every three years.[3] These exemptions exist to protect legal, fair uses of copyrighted materials.

In 2006, University of Pennsylvania film professor Peter DeCherney received a special exemption from the Copyright Office, one that enabled film professors to legally unlock the CSS technology on DVDs.[4] But, the exemption was limited: Only film professors were eligible to use the exemption, and only for the disks housed in the department's film library.

In 2009, a variety of librarians, educators, and advocates gathered to request that that the exemption for film professors be extended to include other educators. Teachers of science, history, medicine, law, and the humanities all find film to be a powerful tool for teaching and learning. K–12 teachers in English, social studies, and health want to use film clips to teach critical analysis and communication skills. That's why I participated, on behalf of media literacy educators and their students. Why should film professors be the only educators who can use film for educational purposes?

Current copy-protection technology on DVDs restricts practices that are reasonably construed as falling under the doctrine of fair use. Right now, DRM restrictions make it impossible for educators to make a transformative use of copyrighted material.

Media literacy educators' use of copyrighted materials is inherently transformative because the use of copyrighted content is not for the same intrinsic purpose as the one the copyright owner intended. Rather, the copyrighted content is used to:

- illustrate key concepts of media literacy;
- deconstruct and critically analyze media messages;
- identify specific production techniques employed in commercial motion pictures or TV shows;
- explore economic, political, social, or cultural values represented; or
- help build skills and knowledge through the creation of student-produced works to demonstrate those ideas and techniques.

William Costanzo, a Professor of English and Film at Westchester Community College (State University of New York), authored a leading writing composition textbook for college students titled *The Writer's Eye: Composition in the Multimedia Age.*[5] In a typical class, he may need to compare excerpts from several movies or television shows. His writing composition and film students may be examining the changing images of women in television, for example, or the evolution of American film comedy.

In previous years, he might have cued up several videocassettes to relevant scenes and screened them in succession so that his students could explore the shifting patterns of speech, dress, and behavior that signify shifting cultural values. Or, he might have used a laser disc to jump from one scene in a movie to another to discover how a character develops or a theme is played out. The linear technology of videocassettes and the digital precision of laser discs permitted this kind of close analysis.

However, with the advent of DVDs, such standard classroom practices have become extremely difficult if not impossible. Most DVDs do not allow the user to locate a precise frame in the film. At best, users are limited to preselected "chapters," so a teacher must resort to clumsy forwarding techniques to find a scene she wants to focus on.

To show a series of film clips in succession, users must start each film from the beginning. To make matters worse, many DVDs force users to endure many minutes of advertising and promotional material before they can even start the film. Often, it is impossible to skip this material—the best you can do is fast forward through it.

The DMCA law has become a major obstacle to effective education. As Costanzo himself explains,

> Imagine an English teacher who wants to trace the character development of Iago in *Othello* or who wants to compare the tragic heroes in three Shakespearean plays. A similar copyright restriction on print materials would require the teacher to start each play anew, read the preface, and then flip through the pages searching for each relevant quote.[6]

All this delay and technical maneuvering frustrates the educational objectives of a lesson, and it discourages educators from using films as educational tools.

Why couldn't teachers use older media, such as VHS, which are not encrypted using digital-rights management copy-control systems? While some of us treasure our old VHS copies, the VHS format is becoming less and less effective. It's no longer possible to find contemporary film works in VHS format. The very last batch of VHS blank tapes was shipped in 2008. Many teachers and most students do not even have a VHS player/recorder in their homes. Sadly, some educators keep using old VHS tapes (even when the content has outlived its usefulness) just because they can't effectively access more current films. That's not good for either students or teachers. *The use of relevant and contemporary texts, tools, and technologies helps educators to make meaningful connections between the classroom and the culture.*

The Ironies Resulting From Technology Shift

Right now, educators are struggling: The old technologies for capturing media material (like VHS) are gone, and the new technologies are locked up. Many teachers threw out their home VHS machines years ago, when they got their flat-screen TVs. In most schools, VCRs have been replaced with DVD players. And in most K–12 classrooms, most teachers can't access the video content that's available through YouTube or other video-sharing sites. Internet filtering software in schools literally "locks up" social media resources that could be used quite productively for teaching and learning.

It's truly ironic that the digital technology shift, while making diverse content more available to students and teachers as consumers at home, has also made it harder for teachers to make use of that content to build active critical thinking in responding to mass media, popular culture, and digital media.

Teachers deeply respect the rights of copyright owners and want to be lawful. In our research, we found that the large majority of teachers are not bypassing CSS technology because it's not lawful to do so. But they want for themselves and their students the right to exercise their legal rights to use copyrighted materials under the doctrine of fair use.

Sharing media has become "natural" for students—they have grown up with the practice of routinely copying music, video, and software to use on their multiple screens and devices. Rather than berate them with oversimplistic messages that equate all forms of sharing with stealing, it is preferable to teach students that some forms of sharing are fair and legal and other forms of sharing are unfair and illegal. Students can learn to recognize and make distinctions between pirating and fair use.

Copyright law offers strong protection to both owners and users. An exemption to the DMCA law that permits educators to bypass CSS encryption will help educators and students strengthen their respect for their rights and responsibilities under copyright law. Without such an exemption, respect for copyright law will continue to erode.

In Pennsylvania, we have begun teaching library media specialists and technology integration specialists about copyright and fair use, with support from the Classrooms for the Future program at the Pennsylvania Department of Education, using the ideas, resources, and materials found in this book. See the detailed outline that's included in Resource A at the back of this book. When teachers find out the story is not what they expected—it's not all "no, no, no"—they are very receptive to teaching about copyright.

If a DMCA exemption is granted to permit educators and their students to make legal excerpts of movie clips, it provides a "teachable moment" for distinguishing between pirating and fair use.

An Impractical Alternative

At the U.S. Copyright Office hearings in May 2009, the media industry lawyers began their argument by saying that (of course) educators are entitled to make fair use of DVD content. But it doesn't have to be easy or convenient for them. That's not what the law mandates.

So instead of enabling educators and students to bypass CSS for educational purposes, they propose bizarre alternatives to bypassing CSS, like screen capture—this means videotaping a TV set while it's playing a DVD.

The industry lawyers even showed an educational video on how to do this with a $900 video camera, a lot of special cords, a flat screen TV, and a perfectly darkened room. But I've tried it myself, and it's not a practical strategy. Where can you find a perfectly darkened, perfectly quiet room in a public school? I have never seen one. In addition, K–12 classroom teachers, who are in the classroom with students for five hours per day, generally don't have time for such a complicated procedure. Many will also not have the money, time, or skill— these are barriers, too.

The Future of Intellectual Property: Three Views

Educators need to use multimedia resources and content effectively to build these 21st-century learning skills:

- Creativity
- Collaboration
- Critical thinking
- Communication

We live in a world where content comes to us seamlessly from our computers. Teachers and students need to be able to use digital media in just the same ways we now use and quote from news articles, books, and other resources—easily and fluidly, at the touch of a keystroke.

There's no doubt about it: We're in the middle of a set of rapid cultural changes that are the result of widespread access to the Internet and other information technologies. These changes are setting the stage for a vigorous discussion about the role of copyright and fair use in contemporary society.

The human need to share, it seems, is powerful. The Internet is appealing to us as educators because it's virtually stuffed with examples of academic, informational, and expressive work of all sorts, which has been developed by people who are making and sharing materials freely. As resources like Wikipedia, Flickr, and many other Web sites demonstrate, people create new ideas and information because they're motivated by something *more* than just the desire for profit.

At the same time, both large media companies and independent artists who are trying to make a living from their creative work are asserting their rights to control information and profit from it. What are the implications for the future of copyright? Let's consider three perspectives on the future of intellectual property, each of which calls for a different course of action.

1. Create a New Model of Licensing: Some Rights Reserved

One new model for copyright is the licensing of creative works under the Creative Commons model. As we learned in Chapter 1, Creative Commons promotes itself as a best-of-both-worlds way for creators to protect their works while encouraging certain uses of them.[7] The Creative Commons model allows creators to specify exactly how they want their work to be used by others—in other words, they can declare "some rights reserved."

Creative Commons was developed in order to counteract the problems with the current copyright system—namely, the fact that large copyright holders were exercising a disproportionate amount of power that made it hard for new content creators to distribute their work. Larry Lessig, the Harvard Law School professor who developed the concept, has publicly condemned the "permissions culture" that is evident in the current copyright system. In his book *Free Culture* (published under a Creative Commons license and available free online), he writes,

> The law's response to the Internet, when tied to changes in the technology of the Internet itself, has massively increased the effective regulation of creativity in America. To build upon or critique the culture around us one must ask, Oliver Twist–like, for permission first. Permission is, of course, often granted— but it is not often granted to the critical or the independent. We have built a kind of cultural nobility; those within the noble class live easily; those outside it don't.[8]

Creative Commons offers alternatives to this permission culture with new types of licenses for creators who wish to share their work. There are searchable indexes for users who are looking to find work that is freely available.

While Lessig and other scholars argue that Creative Commons provides a useful copyright alternative, the model has received some criticism. For example, the Creative Commons model is based on the same corporate economic system as copyright—with a focus on author's rights.

Other critics claim that Creative Commons is providing unnecessary licenses, and that some of the Creative Commons licensing options are incompatible with one another. Finally, others argue that Creative Commons licenses actually diminish users' rights by promoting a system of licensing options instead of taking advantage of the doctrine of fair use.

2. Reclaim Fair Use With Advocacy From Communities of Practice

Peter Jaszi and Patricia Aufderheide are part of a movement to reclaim freedom of expression under copyright law. They recognize that copyright law has been reframed in the last several decades in order to benefit large media conglomerates and, as a result, has diminished the quality and quantity of work available in the public domain. According to Aufderheide, corporations have "zealously pursued their ownership rights and worked to intimidate and misinform potential users and the general public about the viability of the doctrine of fair use."[9]

The solution: Educate communities of practice about intellectual property and their rights under the doctrine of fair use. Judges have shown us that the doctrine of fair use can only be applied by considering the social practices within creative communities. Artists, teachers, architects, TV producers, and poets all have social norms, established by the traditions within each professional group, for what's appropriate in using copyrighted materials.

These social norms exist side by side with the marketplace model for disseminating information and entertainment. Because copyright law includes a provision for fair use that is flexible and contextual, it can be responsive to the social norms of many different creative communities.

In this view, copyright law is an effective way to ensure the development of innovative ideas and the spread of knowledge. The rights of the copyright holder must be respected, but the rights of users must be equally respected so that people can use copyrighted material in new and innovative ways. The "best practices" approach can help creative communities advocate for a robust interpretation of fair use, which enables the law to be relevant to the new forms of usage, sharing, and distribution that are now part of daily life in a networked information society.

But some critics of this approach say it's just too mainstream: It doesn't depend on making radical changes to copyright law, and merely exploits an existing facet of the law. It's based on the potentially questionable premise that people, once informed about copyright and fair use, will become stakeholders in advocating their rights under the law. But will they?

3. Declare Copyright Unnecessary in a 21st-Century Information Economy

Legal scholar Yochai Benkler writes about the future of copyright in a networked society. He believes that nonmarket information production (that is, the free creation of information that is unencumbered by ownership rights) may be superior to the traditional industrial model that emphasizes exclusive rights.

Perhaps the economic model of information as a commodity might not be the best fit for an information society. After all, economists consider information to be a special kind of property. As I explained in Chapter 1, cultural products are not like other kinds of property because if one person consumes it, there is no effect on whether or not another person can consume it as well. Nonmarket sharing of culture (like music and storytelling, for example) is the way much culture has been shared throughout history, until just very recently.[10]

Benkler believes that the current economic model of classifying intellectual property as a marketable product is simply inefficient.[11] Right now, the current market system attempts to put a price on these resources and thereby restricts access to them. People who wish to freely share information, culture, and knowledge are being systematically shut down by corporations that have an economic interest in controlling the production and dissemination of information and entertainment.

This makes access to creative works more difficult to access and more expensive for the general public. This is not efficient from either an economic standpoint or a cultural one.

The growth of a nonmarket production system that encourages the free flow of information, knowledge, and culture would intensify the spread of knowledge and innovation.

After all, the cost of creating new material is typically much lower in a production model that relies on sharing information. We have seen a tremendous growth in the number of successful collaborative, peer-production projects where creative products are developed outside of the traditional economic system. It does not require a huge financial investment to create on the Web. Open source software, social sharing, and other forms of peer production are widespread today.

However, as we have seen in this chapter, industries with an economic interest in maintaining the proprietary model of information dissemination (for example, Hollywood and the music industry) are working towards more restrictive copyright legislation that could shut down many peer-production and information sharing projects.

In Benkler's view, overly strict international and American copyright laws are obstacles to the free flow of information.[12] Copyright has become more hostile to users' rights. Fair use has been narrowed, criminal penalties are in effect for many peer-to-peer sharing projects, and some large corporations are attempting to halt information sharing with high licensing fees or legal intimidation.

Are intellectual property laws, copyrights, and patents still useful ways to regulate information in a world in which information consumers are now users and creators themselves? Benkler notes,

> If we pass a law that regulates information production too strictly, allowing its beneficiaries to impose prices that are too high on today's innovators, then we will have not only too little consumption of information today, but also too little production of new information tomorrow.[13]

As part of a staff development program, one group of teachers in Pennsylvania, who were learning about copyright and fair use, explored the similarities and differences between these different views, and Figure 5.1 shows their analysis.

When we encounter these three visions of intellectual property, we can see why the copyright issue has gained so much traction in the public sphere recently. Copyright matters. Consider which of these views of copyright best matches your sense of what's needed for the future of our society.

All these ideas are circulating in our culture today and our perspectives on these issues are a significant part of the mix. As educators, we need to be leaders, not followers, in the public discourse about copyright and fair use.

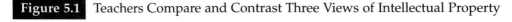

Figure 5.1 Teachers Compare and Contrast Three Views of Intellectual Property

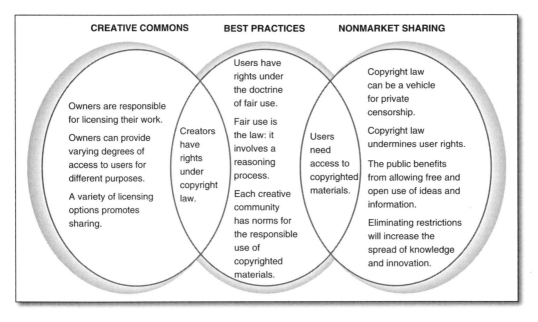

| CREATIVE COMMONS | BEST PRACTICES | NONMARKET SHARING |

Owners are responsible for licensing their work.

Owners can provide varying degrees of access to users for different purposes.

A variety of licensing options promotes sharing.

Creators have rights under copyright law.

Users have rights under the doctrine of fair use.

Fair use is the law: it involves a reasoning process.

Each creative community has norms for the responsible use of copyrighted materials.

Users need access to copyrighted materials.

Copyright law can be a vehicle for private censorship.

Copyright law undermines user rights.

The public benefits from allowing free and open use of ideas and information.

Eliminating restrictions will increase the spread of knowledge and innovation.

What's at Stake: The Future of Education

Because powerful, easy-to-use digital technology sits in the homes of most children and young people in our schools, students are growing up in a world where knowledge, entertainment, and information is at their fingertips, on the many different screens in their lives.

But what are they learning about their rights and responsibilities when it comes to these tools?

To be a citizen of the information age, there is a set of knowledge and skills that needs to be learned beginning in elementary school and continuing through graduate school. As this book reveals, learning about copyright and fair use is an important part of *digital citizenship*.

Critical analysis of media texts, tools, and technologies, and the ability to compose using digital tools for a variety of purposes are some of the fundamental components of 21st-century learning. This work can't just be isolated in technology courses. It has to be part of the overall curriculum: All teachers need to play a part.

In nearly every state in the nation, there are high schools where students in English classes compose a video documentary in order to develop research skills and explore the composition process. There are middle school health classes where students learn to critically analyze alcohol and tobacco advertising and explore the glamorized representation of substance abuse in popular movies. There are elementary school children who examine superheroes and celebrities, looking at how their characters are carefully constructed to express a set of values.

Many teachers are exploring how to improve the quality of teaching and learning using technology tools, including Web sites, social networking, cell phones, and other resources. At every grade level and across all the subject areas, creative student-centered multimedia composition projects result from school–community partnerships, district-level initiatives, and the passion and dedication of individual teachers, working in collaboration with enlightened school leaders.

But we must respect the diversity of educational approaches that are developing across the country. In some communities, one-to-one laptop initiatives can accelerate the opportunities for learning by making it possible to use digital media every day in every class for sharing, discussing, analyzing, and creating. In others, educators develop innovative programs that support students' digital learning even without plentiful access to the latest technology.

In every setting, however, the big picture for 21st-century education now must include:

- **Text and Tool Competence:** learning to use texts, tools, and technologies effectively
- **Creativity and Self-Expression:** developing new ideas and new forms of expression
- **Critical Analysis, Problem Solving, and Ethics:** applying critical thinking in responding to information and ideas and making responsible ethical judgments
- **Teamwork and Collaboration:** working together to get things done

I see these practices taking hold in many of the schools that I visit. Why? Thank goodness, good teachers are everywhere.

They are the teachers who care about their students. They love their subjects and want to engage students with active, hands-on learning, using a diverse array of texts, tools, and technologies of the 21st century.

They are the teachers who want to bring meaningful issues and authentic perspectives into the classroom. They want students to consider and reflect upon the stereotypes found in news, advertising, videogames, in novels, and in contemporary movies. They are teachers who want their students to see how historical fact is shaped by the news media as well as through fictional films about historical events. They want to explore literature as a means to share our diverse heritage, examining how culture and values are presented in stories, drama, poetry, TV shows, movies, and more. They are teachers who want students to read and discuss a scientific article to learn how science works as a form of collaborative knowledge creation. They want students to fully participate in their society, taking on the challenges of becoming citizens and not just spectators.

They are teachers who love the Internet and love the library—they want to help their students to be able to evaluate the quality of all the various sorts of information available from many different types of message sources. They are the teachers whose students are invited to collaborate on a meaningful project, applying critical-thinking skills through creative expression, manipulating, reworking and remixing print, sound, image, and digital texts to express themselves, share information, and develop new ideas. They are the teachers whose students use copyrighted content as part and parcel of the learning process.

Such work is not only legal, this book has made the case that it is at the heart of what the copyright law is designed to protect: critical thinking, creative expression, and the spread of knowledge.

Resource A

Leading a Staff Development
Workshop on Copyright and Fair Use

After reading this book, you can use this outline to offer a staff-development program on the topic of copyright and fair use in education, with a particular focus on the use of digital media technologies. The outline below is appropriate for a 90-minute session. This program uses a combination of lecture, activity, viewing and discussion, and small-group work. Downloadable presentation slides and videos are available at www.mediaeducationlab.com/copyright-clarity

Outline

I. Introduction to Copyright Matters for Digital Learning

1. Literacy is expanding as a result of changes in communications technology. Review the four components of 21st-century skills: tool competence; creativity and expression; teamwork and collaboration; and analysis, critical thinking, and ethical judgment. All teachers are responsible for supporting the development of these skills. One component of digital citizenship is understanding copyright and fair use.

2. How confident are you about copyright and fair use?

   Ask participants to reflect on their level of confidence in their knowledge about copyright and fair use as it applies to teaching and learning, using a five-point scale. Are they very confident, somewhat confident, in the middle, not confident, or not at all confident? Invite participants to self-assess and identify their levels of confidence by asking folks to raise their hands or put fingers in the air.

3. The explosion of new communication technologies makes it easy for people to share, use, copy, modify, distribute, and excerpt or quote from preexisting sources. But owners are forcefully asserting their own rights to restrict, limit, charge high fees, discourage use, and they sometimes use scare tactics. Many educators are familiar with the warning labels on DVDs that say "For Home Use Only" and the signs posted in front of copy machines.

4. Activity: What is the purpose of copyright?

   a. Pair-share: Participants discuss their answers to this question with a partner. Allow four minutes for discussion.

   b. Presenter invites a summary of responses: How many included reference to "owners' rights," "making money," or "profit"? Most will raise their hands. How many included references to creativity or the spread of knowledge? Few or none will raise hands.

   c. What's the purpose of copyright? To promote creativity, innovation, and the spread of knowledge. Source: Article 1, Section 8 of the U.S. Constitution, written in 1787.

   d. Question for reflection: Why is our understanding of copyright so distorted? (If time permits, partners can discuss.)

5. Copyright confusion is common not only among educators but also across all sectors of society. Research has shown that there are three types of attitudes common among educators. They include "see no evil"—those who choose to remain ignorant about the law; "close the door"—those who do what they want inside their classrooms but do not share or inform others; and "hypercompliant"—those who follow the "rules" religiously, sometimes applying the rules more vigorously to their colleagues or students than to themselves.

   a. Do educators recognize any or all of these three common attitudes in themselves?

   b. What are the consequences of holding these attitudes? Innovation and creativity in using digital media is reduced; the sharing and spread of innovative practices is limited.

6. Educational-use guidelines contribute to increased, not decreased, copyright confusion among educators.

   a. Charts and graphs that claim you can use 10% of this or 1,000 words of that—educational-use guidelines—are not the law. These come from documents like the *Agreement on Guidelines for Classroom Copyright in Not-for-Profit Institutions*, *Fair Use Guidelines for Educational Multimedia*, and the *Guidelines for the Educational Use of Music*[1]—all of these are negotiated agreements between lawyers representing publishing companies and lawyers representing educational groups. They are not the law.

   b. Quote from Kenneth Crews, director of the Copyright Office at Columbia University:

      The documents created by these negotiated agreements give them the appearance of positive law. These qualities are merely illusory; consequently, the guidelines have had a seriously detrimental effect. They interfere with an actual understanding of the law and erode confidence in the law as created by Congress and the courts.[2]

II. Understanding Copyright and Fair Use

1. In order to ensure that copyright law did not become a form of private censorship, the Copyright Law of 1976 includes Section 107, the doctrine of fair use. Fair use is an exemption—a type of "user right" that limits the rights of the copyright holder, allowing users to make copies without permission or payment under certain conditions. According to Carrie Russell, author of *Complete Copyright*,

   It not only allows but encourages socially beneficial uses of copyrighted works such as teaching, learning, and scholarship. Without fair use, those beneficial uses— quoting from copyrighted works, providing multiple copies to students in class, creating new knowledge based on previously published knowledge—would be infringements. Fair use if the means for assuring a robust and vigorous exchange of copyrighted information.[3]

2. Video Viewing and Discussion: To clarify how fair use applies to media literacy educators, the *Code of Best Practices in Fair Use*

for Media Literacy Education[4] was created. A video is available online. After viewing, discuss these questions:

    a. Why is copyright important to those who promote media literacy?

    b. How is fair use defined in the video?

    c. What are the benefits to having a code of best practices?

3. Pass out copies of the *Code of Best Practices for Fair Use in Media Literacy Education.* Review the five principles of the Code (pp. 10–13). Educators can:

    a. make copies of newspaper articles, TV shows, and other copyrighted works and use them and keep them for educational use;

    b. create curriculum materials and scholarship with copyrighted materials embedded; and

    c. share, sell, and distribute curriculum materials with copyrighted materials embedded.

Students can:

    a. use copyrighted works in creating new material; and

    b. distribute their works digitally if they meet the transformativeness standard.

4. Note that each of these principles comes with a description, rationale, and limitations. That's because users need to make fair-use determinations based on the unique features of the specific context and situation. The five principles reflect the consensus of the educational community who created it—but the *Code* does not replace the need for critical thinking and reasoned judgment. By providing a deep context for understanding copyright and fair use, the *Code of Best Practices* increases educators' understanding of the law.

5. Discuss the concept of transformativeness, which occurs when people add value or repurpose copyrighted material to create something new.

    a. Review facts of the case *Bill Graham Archives v. Dorling Kindersley Ltd.* on pages 44–47 of this book to show why the courts considered the publisher's for-profit use of the poster images to be a fair use.

    b. Video Viewing and Discussion: Play the *Schoolhouse Rock*–style music video, "Users' Rights, Section 107." The video is available online (www.mediaeducationlab.com/2-user-rights-section-107-music-video), and the song lyrics are shown on page 79. Discuss: How is transformativeness defined in this video? Why is context and situation so important in making a determination of fair use?

6. The *Code of Best Practices* is now the official fair-use policy of the National Council of Teachers of English, the national association of more than 60,000 English teachers. Here's why the *Code of Best Practices* helps.

   a. It helps educates educators themselves understand how fair use applies to own work.

   b. It persuades gatekeepers, including school leaders, librarians, and technology specialists, to accept well-founded assertions of fair use.

   c. It promotes revisions to school policies regarding the use of copyrighted materials in education.

   d. It may discourage copyright owners from threatening or bringing lawsuits.

   e. In the unlikely event that such suits were brought, it may provide the defendant with a basis to show that his or her uses were both objectively reasonable and undertaken in good faith.

   The *Code of Best Practices* can help increase teachers' confidence in making a fair-use determination about the use of copyrighted materials to build students' critical thinking and communication skills.

III. Making a Determination of Fair Use

1. Fair use requires reasoning and critical thinking. No rules or guidelines can simplify the decision-making process because a fair-use determination rests on the specific context and situation of the use. Rather than defer to lawyers who may not have a full understanding of the educational goals, context, and situation, it is important for educators themselves to make fair-use determinations.

2. The "reasonableness standard" increases educators' confidence in making a determination of fair use. The copyright law includes a special provision that can eliminate statutory damages for librarians and educators who "reasonably believed

and had reasonable grounds for believing" that his or her use was a fair use.

3. Video: Watch the elementary school case study, available online (www.mediaeducationlab.com/case-study-video-elementary), and discuss these questions:

   a. The teacher in the video claims that the use of images and music in these PSAs was a transformative use. Do you agree? Does the students' work add value and repurpose? Why or why not?

   b. Why do you think these students chose to use copyrighted works in their videos? Why do you think they chose a picture of a Cadillac instead of a generic car image with no logo? How was the use of copyrighted material relevant to the project's learning outcomes?

   c. Which of the five principles of the *Code of Best Practices* are relevant in this case?

4. Jigsaw discussion activity: Participants first break into groups of five to eight, receive a hypothetical case, find others who have the same case, and discuss. Then, they return to their original group and share their reasoning with others. Hypothetical cases can be found online at www.copyright confusion.wikispaces.com. For large groups, it is effective to use color coding to identify the different scenarios. Participants first find others who have the same hypothetical scenario and discuss whether the specific case is a fair use of copyrighted materials. Participants may discover that they need more information about context and situation to analyze the case. Encourage them to invent facts to fill in the missing details. This helps participants recognize that there are often situational nuances to consider in making a fair-use determination.

5. Explain that, for educators who make active use of copyrighted materials in their work, it may be useful to document the fair-use reasoning process. If you have access to online technology, you can demonstrate the use of the Google Docs form (available at: www.copyrightconfusion.wikispaces .com/reasoning-tool).

6. Students can document their fair-use reasoning skills using the form on page 104. This form helps students

reflect on their decision-making process about the use of copyrighted materials as part of their own creative and academic work.

IV. Educators Need to Be Leaders, Not Followers

1. Teaching materials for exploring copyright and fair use with students are available at http://mediaeducationlab.com/code-best-practices-fair-use-media-literacy-education.

2. This presentation is based on a powerful legal theory—when it comes to interpreting how fair use applies to a particular set of practices within a community, the norms and values of people within that community are important. That's why we believe that exercising your fair-use rights makes them stronger.

3. Since educators are both "authors" and "users" of intellectual property, we understand how important it is for educators themselves to advocate for teaching digital citizenship. Copyright and fair use are fundamental components of this work: Respecting the rights of both authors and users is an essential life skill for participatory culture.

V. Time for Questions and Answers

1. Educators will ask questions that begin, "Is it OK for me or my students to . . . ?" and describe a specific situation. Resist the tendency to answer with your own determination of fair use. When you offer the "answer," it doesn't promote critical thinking on the part of the educator. Encourage the questioner to answer his or her own question by using reasoning and judgment to make a fair-use determination, answering the two critical questions:

   a. Did the use of copyrighted material "transform" the material by using it for a different purpose than that of the original, or did it just repeat the work with the same intent and value as the original?

   b. Was the material taken appropriate in kind and in amount, considering the nature of the copyrighted work and the use?

   Remind teachers that, as they practice, they will gain confidence in using their "fair use" muscles as a part of the critical-thinking process.

Document the Fair-Use Reasoning Process

Student Name:

Project Title:

What is the purpose of your project?

Who is the target audience?

What techniques are you using to attract and hold attention?

Your Use of Copyrighted Material

I am using (description of resource used)

because (provide a reason here)

Provide a full citation of the resource:

Did your use of the work "transform" the material taken from the copyrighted work by using it for a different purpose than that of the original? Explain why your work does not just repeat the intent and value of the original source material.

Did you use only the amount you needed to accomplish your purpose? Explain why made your selection.

Complete these questions for each of the copyrighted resource materials you use in your project.

Resource B

Excerpts From Copyright Law

Copyright in the Constitution

Government can establish a copyright system to "promote the progress of science and useful arts, by securing for limited times to authors and inventors the exclusive right to their respective writings and discoveries."

—Section 1, Article 8, U.S. Constitution, 1787

The Copyright Act of 1976, Section 107

The fair use of a copyrighted work is not an infringement of copyright. This includes reproduction in copies for purposes such as criticism, comment, news reporting, teaching (including multiple copies for classroom use), scholarship, or research. In determining whether the use made of a work in any particular case is a fair use, the factors to be considered shall include

- The purpose and character of the use, including whether such use is of a commercial nature or is for nonprofit educational purposes;
- The nature of the copyrighted work;
- The amount and substantiality of the portion used in relation to the copyrighted work as a whole; and
- The effect of the use upon the potential market for or value of the copyrighted work.

Digital Millennium Copyright Act of 1998, Section 1201

The Digital Millennium Copyright Act (DMCA) makes it illegal to produce technology, devices, or services that circumvent access to copyrighted works. It also criminalizes the act of circumventing content, whether or not there is actual infringement of copyright itself. Section 1201 gives the Register of Copyrights the power to grant three-year exemptions for some forms of circumvention.

Circumvention of Copyright-Protection Systems

(A) No person shall circumvent a technological measure that effectively controls access to a work protected under this title. The prohibition contained in the preceding sentence shall take effect at the end of the 2-year period beginning on the date of the enactment of this chapter.

(B) The prohibition contained in subparagraph (A) shall not apply to persons who are users of a copyrighted work which is in a particular class of works, if such persons are, or are likely to be in the succeeding 3-year period, adversely affected by virtue of such prohibition in their ability to make noninfringing uses of that particular class of works under this title, as determined under subparagraph (C).

(C) During the 2-year period described in subparagraph (A), and during each succeeding 3-year period, the Librarian of Congress, upon the recommendation of the Register of Copyrights, who shall consult with the Assistant Secretary for Communications and Information of the Department of Commerce and report and comment on his or her views in making such recommendation, shall make the determination in a rulemaking proceeding for purposes of subparagraph (B) of whether persons who are users of a copyrighted work are, or are likely to be in the succeeding 3-year period, adversely affected by the prohibition under subparagraph (A) in their ability to make noninfringing uses under this title of a particular class of copyrighted works. In conducting such rulemaking, the Librarian shall examine—

(i) The availability for use of copyrighted works;

(ii) The availability for use of works for nonprofit archival, preservation, and educational purposes;

(iii) The impact that the prohibition on the circumvention of technological measures applied to copyrighted works has on criticism, comment, news reporting, teaching, scholarship, or research;

(iv) The effect of circumvention of technological measures on the market for or value of copyrighted works; and

(v) Such other factors as the Librarian considers appropriate.

2002 TEACH ACT, Section 110

Section 110(1) offers educators a special exemption for displaying or using copyrighted materials for face-to-face learning, while Section 110(2) ("The Teach Act") enables educators to share materials on digital networks for distance learning. These exemptions should not be confused with the fair use provision, which offers as an independent basis for exemption from copyright infringement liability.

Exemptions for Certain Performances and Displays

Notwithstanding the provisions of section 106, the following are not infringements of copyright:

Section 110(1) : performance or display of a work by instructors or pupils in the course of face-to-face teaching activities of a nonprofit educational institution, in a classroom or similar place devoted to instruction, unless, in the case of a motion picture or other audiovisual work, the performance, or the display of individual images, is given by means of a copy that was not lawfully made under this title, and that the person responsible for the performance knew or had reason to believe was not lawfully made;

Section 110(2): except with respect to a work produced or marketed primarily for performance or display as part of mediated instructional activities transmitted via digital networks, or a performance or display that is given by means of a copy or phonorecord that is not lawfully made and acquired under this title, and the transmitting government body or accredited nonprofit educational institution knew or had reason to believe was not lawfully made and acquired, the performance of a nondramatic literary or musical work or reasonable and limited portions of any other work, or display of a work in an amount comparable to that which is typically displayed in the course of a live classroom session, by or in the course of a transmission, if—

(A) the performance or display is made by, at the direction of, or under the actual supervision of an instructor as an integral part of a class session offered as a regular part of the systematic mediated instructional activities of a governmental body or an accredited nonprofit educational institution; (B) the performance or display is directly related and of material assistance to the teaching content of the transmission; (C) the transmission is made solely for, and, to the extent technologically feasible, the reception of such transmission is limited to students officially enrolled in the course for which the transmission is made. . . .

And in the case of digital transmissions—applies technological measures that reasonably prevent retention of the work in accessible form by recipients of the transmission from the transmitting body or institution for longer than the class session; and unauthorized further dissemination of the work in accessible form by such recipients to others; and does not engage in conduct that could reasonably be expected to interfere with technological measures used by copyright owners to prevent such retention or unauthorized further dissemination;

. . . . In paragraph (2), the term "mediated instructional activities" with respect to the performance or display of a work by digital transmission under this section refers to activities that use such work as an integral part of the class experience, controlled by or under the actual supervision of the instructor and analogous to the type of performance or display that would take place in a live classroom setting. The term does not refer to activities that use, in 1 or more class sessions of a single course, such works as textbooks, course packs, or other material in any media, copies or phonorecords of which are typically purchased or acquired by the students in higher education for their independent use and retention or are typically purchased or acquired for elementary and secondary students for their possession and independent use. . . .

For purposes of paragraph (2), accreditation (A) with respect to an institution providing post-secondary education, shall be as determined by a regional or national accrediting agency recognized by the Council on Higher Education Accreditation or the United States Department of Education; and (B) with respect to an institution providing elementary or secondary education, shall be as recognized by the applicable state certification or licensing procedures.

For purposes of paragraph (2), no governmental body or accredited nonprofit educational institution shall be liable for infringement by reason of the transient or temporary storage of material carried out through the automatic technical process of a digital transmission of the performance or display of that material as authorized under paragraph (2). No such material stored on the system or network controlled or operated by the transmitting body or institution under this paragraph shall be maintained on such system or network in a manner ordinarily accessible to anyone other than anticipated recipients.

No such copy shall be maintained on the system or network in a manner ordinarily accessible to such anticipated recipients for a longer period than is reasonably necessary to facilitate the transmissions for which it was made. . . .

Resources for Learning More About Copyright and Fair Use

Complete Copyright: An Everyday Guide for Librarians by Carrie Russell (2004)

This comprehensive guide addresses copyright issues, including fair use, the TEACH Act, the Digital Millennium Copyright Act, Internet-related issues, and advocacy in an accessible yet comprehensive format. Available at http://www.alastore.ala.org/.

Copyright Law for Librarians and Educators by Kenneth Crews (2006)

This reference book provides an introduction to the fundamentals of current copyright law, helping educators and librarians keep abreast of changes in copyright law and fair use. Available at http://www.alastore.ala.org/.

The Wealth of Networks: How Social Production Transforms Markets and Freedom by Yochai Benkler (2006)

Benkler reviews the changing nature of knowledge production in contemporary society and argues that communications networks are reshaping our understanding of the concepts of intellectual property and the economics of information. More information available at http://www.benkler.org.

Freedom of Expression: Resistance and Repression in the Age of Intellectual Property by Kembrew McLeod (2007)

This engaging documentary explores how intellectual property laws are used as tools of censorship, restricting the public's access to information. Available at http://www.mediaed.org.

Copyright and Fair Use Podcasts

These free podcasts feature Professor Kenneth Crews explaining fair-use principles in detail in an engaging way. Available at http://www.lifeofalawstudent.com/category/podcasters/prof-kenneth-crews/.

Center for Social Media

The Center for Social Media at American University showcases and analyzes strategies to use media as creative tools for public knowledge and action. They have conducted extensive work on fair use for creative communities. Available at http://www.centerforsocialmedia.org.

Creative Commons

Creative Commons is a nonprofit organization that has developed a new licensing model that allows creators to specify which rights they wish to reserve in order to promote sharing of creative work. More information available at http://creativecommons.org.

Media Education Lab

Music videos, video case studies, and lesson plans developed by the author of this book help students learn about copyright and fair use in ways that strengthen reading, critical thinking, and communications skills. Available at http://www.mediaeducationlab.com.

Electronic Frontier Foundation

A non-profit organization that defends free speech, privacy, innovation, and consumer rights in the digital environment. "Teaching Copyright" offers lesson plans for exploring piracy, file sharing, and fair use. Available at: http://teachingcopyright.org.

Endnotes

Acknowledgments

1. Russell, C. (2004). *Complete copyright: An everyday guide for librarians.* Washington, DC: American Library Association, Office for Information Technology Policy. (p. 19).

Chapter 1

1. Hobbs, R. (2005). Media literacy and the K–12 content areas. In G. Schwarz & P. U. Brown (Eds.), *Media literacy: Transforming curriculum and teaching* (pp. 74–99). National Society for the Study of Education, Yearbook 104. Malden, MA: Blackwell.

2. Hobbs, R. (2007). *Reading the media: Media literacy in high school English.* New York: Teachers College Press.

3. Arnett, J. J. (Ed.). (2007). *Encyclopedia of children, adolescents and the media.* Thousand Oaks, CA: Sage.

4. Ibid.

5. Aufderheide, P., & Firestone, C. (1993). *Media literacy: National leadership conference.* Washington, DC: Aspen Institute. (p. 6).

6. Livingstone, S. (2004). Media literacy and the challenge of new information and communication technologies. *The Communication Review 7*, 3–14. (p. 5).

7. Hobbs, R. (2004). A review of school-based initiatives in media literacy. *American Behavioral Scientist, 48*(1), 48–59.

8. Hobbs, R., Jaszi, P., & Aufderheide, P. (2007). *The cost of copyright confusion for media literacy.* Washington, DC: Center for Social Media, American University.

9. Scheibe, C. (2008, May 7). Personal interview.

10. Hobbs, R., Jaszi, P., & Aufderheide, P. (2007). *The cost of copyright confusion for media literacy.* Washington, DC: Center for Social Media, American University. (p. 4).

11. Ibid. (p. 4).

12. Baker, F. (2008, February 1). Personal interview.

13. Rogow, F. (2008, May 7). Personal interview.

14. Hobbs, R., Jaszi, P., & Aufderheide, P. (2007). *The cost of copyright confusion for media literacy.* Washington, DC: Center for Social Media, American University. (p. 5).

15. Crews, K. (1993). *Copyright, fair use, and the challenge for universities: Promoting the progress of higher education.* Chicago: University of Chicago Press.

16. Valenza, J. (2008, April 1). Fair use and transformativness: It may shake your world. *School Library Journal.* Retrieved December 24, 2009, from http://www.schoollibraryjournal.com/blog/1340000334/post/1420024142.html?q=transformativeness

17. Ibid. (para. 22).

18. American University Center for Social Media, Media Education Lab at Temple University, and Washington College of Law, Program on Intellectual Property and the Public Interest. (2008). *Code of best practices in fair use for media literacy education.* Washington, DC: Center for Social Media, American University. Retrieved January 2, 2009, from http://www.centerforsocialmedia.org/resources/publications/code_for_media_literacy_education

Chapter 2

1. Copyright law of the United States. Title 17 of the U.S. Code. Retrieved December 24, 2009, from http://www.copyright.gov/title17

2. Joyce, C., Leaffer, M., Jaszi, P., & Ochoa, T. (2003). *Copyright law* (6th ed.). Newark, NJ: Lexis Nexis. (p. 54).

3. Hoskinson, J. (Director). (2009). Episode #05004: Lawrence Lessig [Television series episode]. In S. Colbert & A. Silverman (Executive producers), The Colbert Report. New York, NY: Comedy Central. Retrieved January 8, 2010, from http://www.colbertnation.com/the-colbert-report-videos/215454/january-08-2009/lawrence-lessig

4. *Columbia World of Quotations.* (1996). New York: Columbia University Press. Available from http://www.bartleby.com

5. Russell, C. (2004). *Complete copyright: An everyday guide for librarians.* Washington, DC: American Library Association, Office for Information Technology Policy. (p. 1).

6. Jaszi, P. (1996). Caught in the net of copyright. Symposium: Innovation and the information environment. *Oregon Law Review, 75,* 299–308.

7. Hobbs, R., Jaszi, P., & Aufderheide, P. (1998). *Introducing the code of best practices for fair use in media literacy education* [Video recording]. Washington, DC: Center for Social Media, American University.

8. Lessig, L. (2004). *Free culture: How big media uses technology and the law to lock down culture and control creativity.* New York: Penguin.

9. Hobbs, R., Jaszi, P., & Aufderheide, P. (2007). *The cost of copyright confusion for media literacy.* Washington, DC: Center for Social Media, American University. Retrieved January 2, 2009, from http://www .centerforsocialmedia.org/resources/publications/the_cost_of_ copyright_confusion_for_media_literacy

We conducted open-ended, long-form interviews approximately 45 minutes or longer, usually by phone, with 63 educators who were identified as participating in programs that help children, young people, and adults develop critical thinking and communication skills. We sampled to include a balance of educators working in K–12, college and university faculty in media studies/communication, college and university faculty in departments of education, individuals working in nonprofit youth-service organizations, and those involved in media production and distribution, or leaders of membership organizations. We interviewed both seasoned veterans of more than twenty years of media-literacy teaching and educators with three or more years of experience. Interview subjects were recruited through national membership organizations, including the Alliance for a Media Literate America, the Action Coalition for Media Education, the Student Television Network, and the National Council of Teachers of English, and organizations such as National Alliance for Media Arts and Culture and *Youth Media Reporter.*

The interview consisted of open-ended questions organized into three broad categories: (1) how teachers use copyrighted materials in the classroom or other educational settings for educational purposes; (2) how their students use copyrighted materials in their own creative work; and (3) how teachers use copyrighted materials in their curriculum development, materials production, or other creative work. Interviewers were trained by first listening to another researcher conduct an interview and then participating in a detailed debriefing session. Detailed descriptions of responses were written after each interview was completed; they were then analyzed to discover the most common patterns and themes.

10. Hobbs, R., Jaszi, P., & Aufderheide, P. (2008). *Introducing the code of best practices for fair use in media literacy education* [Video recording]. Washington, DC: Center for Social Media, American University.

11. Hobbs, R., Jaszi, P., & Aufderheide, P. (2007). *The cost of copyright confusion for media literacy.* Washington, DC: Center for Social Media, American University. Retrieved January 2, 2009, from http://www .centerforsocialmedia.org/resources/publications/the_cost_of_ copyright_confusion_for_media_literacy (p. 11)

12. Ibid. (p. 12).

13. Ibid. (p. 14).

14. Ibid. (p. 14).

15. Ibid. (p. 20).

16. Ibid. (p. 14).

17. Ibid. (p. 15).

18. Comment made at a focus group interview. (2008, April 25).

19. Hobbs, R., Jaszi, P., & Aufderheide, P. (2007). *The cost of copyright confusion for media literacy.* Washington, DC: Center for Social Media, American University. Retrieved January 2, 2009, from http:// www.centerforsocialmedia.org/resources/publications/the_cost_ of_copyright_confusion_for_media_literacy (p. 19).

20. Ibid. (p. 9).

21. Ibid. (p. 9).

22. Comment made at a focus group. (2007, November 18).

23. Russell, C. (2004). *Complete copyright: An everyday guide for librarians.* Washington, DC: American Library Association, Office for Information Technology Policy.

24. Crews, K. (2001). The law of fair use and the illusion of fair-use guidelines. *The Ohio State Law Journal, 62,* 601–664. (p. 601).

25. Russell, C. (2004). *Complete copyright: An everyday guide for librarians.* Washington, DC: American Library Association, Office for Information Technology Policy. (p. 27).

26. Davidson, H. (2001). *Copyright chart.* Retrieved December 24, 2009, from http://www.halldavidson.net/copyright_chart.pdf

27. Levering, M. (1999). What's right about fair-use guidelines for the academic community? *Journal of the American Society for Information Science, 50*(14), 1313–1319. (p. 1316).

28. Frazier, K. (1999). What's wrong with fair-use guidelines for the academic community? *Journal of the American Society for Information Science 50*(14), 1320–1323. (p. 1321).

29. Ibid. (p. 1321).

30. Teach Act of 2002, 17 U.S.C. 110. Retrieved January 8, 2010 from http://www.copyright.gov/title17/92chap1.html#110

31. Crews, K. (2002). *New copyright law for distance education: The meaning and importance of the TEACH Act.* Chicago: American Library Association. Available from http://www.ala.org/ala/aboutala/offices/wo/woissues/copyrightb/federallegislation/distanceed/distanceeducation.cfm#requirements (para. 34).

32. Ibid. (para. 34).

33. Ibid. (para. 10).

34. Fisher, W., Palfrey, J., McGeveran, W., Harlow, J. Gassser, U., & Jaszi, P. (2006). *The digital learning challenge: Obstacles to educational uses of copyrighted material in the digital age.* Cambridge, MA: The Berkman Center for Internet & Society Research Publication. Retrieved December 24, 2009, from http://cyber.law.harvard.edu/publications/2006/The_Digital_Learning_Challenge

35. Wilk, J. (2008, February 26). Mybytes teaches a little something about copyright, but what? *Yalsa Blog.* American Library Association. Retrieved December 24, 2009, from http://yalsa.ala.org/blog/2008/02/26/mybytes-teaches-teens-a-little-something-about-copyright-but-what (para. 2).

36. Gillespie, T. (2009). Characterizing copyright in the classroom: The cultural work of anti-piracy campaigns. *Communication, Culture, & Critique* 2(3), 274–318.

37. Copyright Clearance Center. (2009). *Copyright basics: The video.* Available from http://216.183.190.29

38. Triplett, W. (2008, March 3). MPAA canines to dog movie pirates: Malaysian authorities help track counterfeiters. *Variety.* Retrieved December 24, 2009, from http://www.variety.com/article/VR1117981782.html?categoryid=20&cs=1&nid=2562 (para. 10).

Chapter 3

1. Allison, P. (2009, January 31). Opening up to fair use. *Teachers teaching teachers.* [Podcast]. Retrieved December 24, 2009, from http://teachersteachingteachers.org/?cat=388

2. Ibid.

3. Tushnet, R. (2004). Copy this essay: How fair use doctrine harms free speech and how copying serves it. *Yale Law Journal, 114,* 535–590.

4. Duncum, P. (1988). To copy or not to copy: A review. *Studies in Art Education* 29(4), 203–210. (p. 209).

5. Jaszi, P. (1991). Toward a theory of copyright: the metamorphosis of "authorship." *Duke Law Journal, 2*, 455–502.

6. Horan, E. (1996). To market: The Dickinson copyright wars. *The Emily Dickinson Journal, 5*(1), 88–120.

7. DK Adult. (2003). *Grateful Dead: The illustrated trip.* New York: Author.

8. Bill Graham Archives v. Dorling Kindersley Ltd., 448 F.3d 605 (2006). (614–615).

9. Leval, P. N. (1990). Toward a fair use standard, 103. *Harvard Law Review,* 1105–1136. (p. 1111).

10. Bill Graham Archives v. Dorling Kindersley Ltd., 448 F.3d 605 (2006). (614–615).

11. Heymann, L. (2008). Everything is transformative: Fair use and reader response. *Columbia Journal of Law and the Arts, 31.* Retrieved December 24, 2009, from http://papers.ssrn.com/sol3/papers.cfm?abstract_id=1148379

12. Ibid.

13. Band, J. (2008, September 29). *How fair use prevailed in the Harry Potter case.* Association of Research Libraries. Retrieved January 7, 2009, from www.arl.org/bm~doc/harrypotterrev2.pdf (para. 1).

14. Warner Bros. Entertainment Inc. and J. K. Rowling v. RDR Books et al., F. Supp.2d 2008 WL 4126736, S.D.N.Y., NO. 07 CIV. 9667 (RPP) (September 8, 2008).

15. Rife, M. (2007). The fair use doctrine: History, application, and implications for (new media) writing teachers. *Computers and Composition 24,* 154–178. (p. 173).

16. Ibid.

17. Russell, C. (2004). *Complete copyright.* Washington, DC: American Library Association. (p. 19).

18. U.S. Copyright Office. (2007). *Copyright law of the United States.* Title 17 of the U.S. Code. Retrieved December 24, 2009, from http://www.copyright.gov/title17

19. Von Loehmann, F. (2009, Febuary 3). YouTube's January fair use massacre. *Electronic Frontier Foundation.* Retrieved December 24, 2009, from http://www.eff.org/deeplinks/2009/01/youtubes-january-fair-use-massacre

20. Kennedy, R. (2009, February 10). Artist sues the AP over the Obama image. *New York Times,* p. C1.

21. Madison, M. (2009, January 21). Fairey, Obama and fair use. *Madisonian.net.* Retrieved December 24, 2009, from http://madisonian.net/2009/01/21/fairey-obama-and-fair-use

Chapter 4

1. American University Center for Social Media, Media Education Lab at Temple University, and Washington College of Law, Program on Intellectual Property and the Public Interest. (2008). *Code of best practices in fair use for media literacy education.* Washington, DC: Center for Social Media, American University. Retrieved January 2, 2009, from http://www.centerforsocialmedia.org/resources/publications/code_for_media_literacy_education

2. Madison, M. (2006). Fair use and social practices. In P. Yu (Ed.), *Intellectual property and information wealth* (pp. 177–198). Westport, CT: Greenwood.

3. Hampton, H. (Producer). (1986). *Eyes on the prize: America's civil rights years* [DVD]. WGBH Boston: Blackside Films.

4. Brauneis, R. (2009). *Copyright and the world's most popular song.* GWU Legal Studies Research Paper No. 1111624. Retrieved December 29, 2009, from http://ssrn.com/abstract=1111624

5. Dames, K. M. (2006, June). Copyright conundrum: Documentaries and rights clearance. *Information Today, 23*(6), 24–26.

6. Aufderheide, P. (2007). How documentary filmmakers overcame their fear of quoting and learned to employ fair use: A tale of scholarship in action. *International Journal of Communication, 1,* 26–36. Retrieved December 24, 2009, from http://www.centerforsocial media.org/files/pdf/ijoc_article_pat.pdf

   Aufderheide, P., & Jaszi, P. (2004). *Untold stories: Creative consequences of the rights clearance culture for documentary filmmakers.* Washington, DC: Center for Social Media, School of Communication, American University. Retrieved February 1, 2009, from http://www .centerforsocialmedia.org/rock/backgrounddocs/printable_rights report.pdf

7. American University Center for Social Media, Association of Independent Video and Filmmakers, & Washington College of Law, Program on Intellectual Property and the Public Interest. (2005). *Documentary filmmakers' statement of best practices in fair use.* Available from http://www.centerforsocialmedia.org/resources/publications/statement_of_best_practices_ in_fair_use

8. Hurt, B. (2006). *Beyond beats and rhymes* [DVD]. Northampton, MA: Media Education Foundation.

9. American University Center for Social Media, Media Education Lab at Temple University, and Washington College of Law, Program on Intellectual Property and the Public Interest. (2008). *Code of best practices in fair use for media literacy education.*Washington, DC: Center for Social Media, American University. Retrieved January 2, 2009, from

http://www.centerforsocialmedia.org/resources/publications/
code_for_media_literacy_education

10. American University Center for Social Media, Association of
    Independent Video and Filmmakers, & Washington College of Law,
    Program on Intellectual Property and the Public Interest. (2005).
    Documentary filmmakers' statement of best practices in fair use. Available
    from http://www.centerforsocialmedia.org/resources/publications/
    statement_of_best_practices_ in_fair_use

11. Hobbs, R. (Producer), RobbGrieco, M. (Composer), & Beatty, G.
    (Animator). (2008). *What's Copyright?* [Video recording]. Philadelphia:
    Media Education Lab, Temple University. Available from http://
    mediaeducationlab.com/1-whats-copyright-music-video

12. Lee, E. (2008). Warming up to user-generated content. *University of
    Illinois Law Review, 5,* 1459–1548.

13. Hobbs, R. (Producer), RobbGrieco, M. (Composer), & Beatty, G.
    (Animator). (2008). *Users' rights, section 107* [Video recording].
    Philadelphia: Media Education Lab, Temple University. Available from
    http://mediaeducationlab.com/2-user-rights-section-107-music-video

14. *Media Education Foundation* (2010). Available from http://www
    .mediaed.org

15. Grant, D. (2009, January 29). Color this area of the law gray. *Wall
    Street Journal,* p. D7.

16. This illustration by David Klein appeared in Grant, D. (2009,
    January 29). Color this area of law gray. *Wall Street Journal.*
    Retrieved January 8, 2010, from http://online.wsj.com/article/
    SB123319795753727521.html

17. Lee, E. (2008). Warming up to user-generated content. *University of
    Illinois Law Review, 5,* 1459–1548.

Chapter 5

1. Hobbs, R. (2009). *Request for copyright exemption.* Submitted to the
   U.S. Copyright Office (Docket No. RM-200–8). Retrieved December
   24, 2009, from http://www.copyright.gov/1201/2008/index.html

2. Electronic Frontier Foundation. (n.d.). *Digital rights management.*
   Available from http://www.eff.org/issues/drm (para. 4).

3. Herman, B., & Gandy, O. (2006). Catch 1201: A legislative history
   and content analysis of DMCA exemption proceedings. *Cardoza Arts
   and Entertainment Law Journal, 24,* 121–190.

4. DeCherney, P. (2007). From fair use to exemption. *Cinema Journal
   46*(2), 120–127.

5. Costanzo, W. (2007). *The writer's eye: Composition in the multimedia age.* New York: McGraw Hill.

6. Costanzo, W. (2008). *Request for copyright exemption, supporting comments for a DMCA exemption for media literacy education.* Submitted to the U.S. Copyright Office on behalf of Professor Renee Hobbs (Docket No. RM 200–8).

7. Copyright Advisory Network. (2008). *Creative Commons and open licenses.* Retrieved June 17, 2009, from http://www.librarycopyright.net/wiki/index.php?title=Creative_Commons_and_Open_Licenses (para. 1).

8. Lessig, L. (2004). *Free culture: How big media uses technology and the law to lock down culture and control creativity.* New York: Penguin. Retrieved January 1, 2010 from http://www.free-culture.cc/freecontent (p. 10).

9. Aufderheide, P. (2007). How documentary filmmakers overcame their fear of quoting and learned to employ fair use: A tale of scholarship in action. *International Journal of Communication 1,* 26–36. Retrieved December 24, 2009, from http://www.centerforsocial media.org/files/pdf/ijoc_article_pat.pdf (p. 27).

10. Benkler, Y. (2006). *The wealth of networks.* New Haven, CT: Yale University Press. (p. 274).

11. Ibid. (p. 393).

12. Ibid. (p. 417).

13. Ibid. (p. 38).

Resource A

1. U.S. Copyright Office. (n.d.). *Reproductions of copyrighted works by educators and librarians.* Circular 21. Retrieved August 27, 2009 from http://www.copyright.gov/circs/circ21.pdf

2. Crews, K. (2001). The law of fair use and the illusion of fair-use guidelines. *The Ohio State Law Journal, 62,* 602–664.

3. Russell, C. (2004). *Complete copyright.* Washington, DC: American Library Association. (p. 27).

4. American University Center for Social Media, Media Education Lab at Temple University, and Washington College of Law, Program on Intellectual Property and the Public Interest. (2008). *Code of best practices in fair use for media literacy education.* Washington, DC: Center for Social Media, American University. Retrieved January 2, 2009, from http://www.centerforsocialmedia.org/resources/publications/code_for_media_literacy_education

References

Allison, P. (2009, January 31). Opening up to fair use. *Teachers teaching teachers* [Podcast]. Retrieved December 24, 2009, from http://teachersteaching teachers.org/?cat=388

American University Center for Social Media, Media Education Lab at Temple University, and Washington College of Law, Program on Intellectual Property and the Public Interest. (2008). *Code of best practices in fair use for media literacy education.* Washington, DC: Center for Social Media, American University. Retrieved January 2, 2009, from http://www.center forsocialmedia.org/resources/publications/code_for_media_literacy_education

American University Center for Social Media, Association of Independent Video and Filmmakers, & Washington College of Law, Program on Intellectual Property and the Public Interest. (2005). *Documentary filmmakers' statement of best practices in fair use.* Washington, DC: Center for Social Media, American University. Retrieved January 20, 2009, from http://www.centerforsocialmedia.org/resources/publications/statement_of_best_practices_in_fair_use

Arnett, J. J. (Ed.). (2007). *Encyclopedia of children, adolescents and the media.* Thousand Oaks, CA: Sage.

Aufderheide, P. (2007). How documentary filmmakers overcame their fear of quoting and learned to employ fair use: A tale of scholarship in action. *International Journal of Communication 1*, 26–36. Retrieved December 24, 2009, from http://www.centerforsocialmedia.org/files/pdf/ijoc_article_pat.pdf

Aufderheide, P., & Firestone, C. (1993). *Media literacy: National leadership conference.* Washington, DC: Aspen Institute.

Aufderheide, P., & Jaszi, P. (2004). *Untold stories: Creative consequences of the rights clearance culture for documentary filmmakers.* Washington, DC: Center for Social Media, School of Communication, American University. Retrieved February 1, 2009, from http://www.centerforsocialmedia.org/rock/backgrounddocs/printable_rightsreport.pdf

Band, J. (2008, September 29). *How fair use prevailed in the Harry Potter case.* Association of Research Libraries. Retrieved January 7, 2009, from www.arl.org/bm~doc/harrypotterrev2.pdf

Benkler, Y. (2006). *The wealth of networks: How social production transforms markets and freedom.* New Haven, CT: Yale University Press.

Bill Graham Archives v. Dorling Kindersley Ltd., 448 F.3d 605 (2006).

Braman, S. (2006). *Change of state: Information, policy and power.* Cambridge: MIT Press.

Brauneis, R. (2009). *Copyright and the world's most popular song.* GWU Legal Studies Research Paper No. 1111624. Retrieved December 29, 2009, from http://ssrn.com/abstract=1111624

Columbia World of Quotations. (1996). New York: Columbia University Press. Available from http://www.bartleby.com

Copyright Act of 1976. *Copyright law of the United States.* Title 17 of the U.S. Code. Retrieved December 24, 2009, from http://www.copyright.gov/title17

Copyright Advisory Network. (2008). Creative Commons and Open Licenses. Retrieved June 17, 2009, from http://www.librarycopyright.net/wiki/index.php?title=Creative_Commons_and_Open_Licenses

Copyright Clearance Center. (2009). *Copyright basics: The video.* Available from http://216.183.190.29

Copyright Law of the United States of America and Related Laws Contained in Title 17 of the *United States Code*, § 504(c)(2) (2003).

Costanzo, W. (2007). *The writer's eye: Composition in the multimedia age.* New York: McGraw Hill.

Costanzo, W. (2008). *Request for copyright exemption, supporting comments for a DMCA exemption for media literacy education.* Submitted to the U.S. Copyright Office on behalf of Professor Renee Hobbs (Docket No. RM 200–8).

Crews, K. (1993). *Copyright, fair use, and the challenge for universities: Promoting the progress of higher education.* Chicago: University of Chicago Press.

Crews, K. (2001). The law of fair use and the illusion of fair-use guidelines. *The Ohio State Law Journal, 62,* 602–664.

Crews, K. (2002). *New copyright law for distance education: The meaning and importance of the TEACH Act.* Chicago: American Library Association. Available from http://www.ala.org/ala/aboutala/offices/wo/woissues/copyrightb/federallegislation/distanceed/distanceeducation.cfm#requirements

Crews, K. (Ed.). (2006). *Copyright law for librarians and educators* (2nd ed.). Chicago: American Library Association.

Dames, K. M. (2006, June). Copyright conundrum: Documentaries and rights clearance. *Information Today, 23*(6), 24–26.

Davidson, H. (2001). *Copyright chart.* Retrieved December 24, 2009, from http://www.halldavidson.net/copyright_chart.pdf

DeCherney, P. (2007). From fair use to exemption. *Cinema Journal, 46*(2), 120–127.

DK Adult. (2003). *Grateful Dead: The illustrated trip.* New York: Author.

Duncum, P. (1988). To copy or not to copy: A review. *Studies in Art Education, 29*(4), 203–210.

Electronic Frontier Foundation. (n.d.). *Digital rights management.* Available from http://www.eff.org/issues/drm

Fisher, W., Palfrey, J., McGeveran, W., Harlow, J. Gassser, U., & Jaszi, P. (2006). *The digital learning challenge: Obstacles to educational uses of copyrighted material in the digital age.* Cambridge, MA: The Berkman Center for Internet & Society Research Publication. Retrieved December 24, 2009, from http://cyber.law.harvard.edu/publications/2006/The_Digital_ Learning_Challenge

Frazier, K. (1999). What's wrong with fair-use guidelines for the academic community? *Journal of the American Society for Information Science, 50*(14), 1320–1323.

Gillespie, T. (2009). Characterizing copyright in the classroom: The cultural work of anti-piracy campaigns. *Communication, Culture, & Critique, 2*(3), 274–318.

Grant, D. (2009, January 29). Color this area of the law gray. *Wall Street Journal,* p. D7.

Hampton, H. (Producer). (1986). *Eyes on the prize: America's civil rights years* [DVD]. WGBH Boston: Blackside Films.

Herman, B., & Gandy, O. (2006). Catch 1201: A legislative history and content analysis of DMCA exemption proceedings. *Cardoza Arts and Entertainment Law Journal, 24,* 121–190.

Heymann, L. (2008). Everything is transformative: Fair use and reader response. *Columbia Journal of Law and the Arts, 31.* Retrieved December 24, 2009, from http://papers.ssrn.com/sol3/papers.cfm?abstract_id=1148379

Hobbs, R. (2004). A review of school-based initiatives in media literacy. *American Behavioral Scientist, 48*(1), 48–59.

Hobbs, R. (2005). Media literacy and the K–12 content areas. In G. Schwarz & P. U. Brown (Eds.), *Media literacy: Transforming curriculum and teaching* (pp. 74–99). National Society for the Study of Education, Yearbook 104. Malden, MA: Blackwell.

Hobbs, R. (2007). *Reading the media: Media literacy in high school English.* New York: Teachers College Press.

Hobbs, R. (2009). *Request for copyright exemption.* Submitted to the U.S. Copyright Office (Docket No. RM-200–8). Retrieved December 24, 2009, from http://www.copyright.gov/1201/2008/index.html

Hobbs, R., Jaszi, P., & Aufderheide, P. (2009). How media literacy educators reclaimed copyright and fair use. *International Journal of Learning and Media 1*(3), 33–48.

Hobbs, R. (Producer), Grieco, M. R. (Composer), & Beatty, G. (Animator). (2008). *Users' rights, section 107* [Video recording]. Philadelphia: Media Education Lab, Temple University. Available from http://mediaeducationlab .com/2-user-rights-section-107-music-video

Hobbs, R., Jaszi, P., & Aufderheide, P. (2008). *Introducing the code of best practices for fair use in media literacy education* [Video recording]. Washington, DC: Center for Social Media, American University. Available from http://mediaeducationlab.com/video-overview

Hobbs, R., Jaszi, P., & Aufderheide, P. (2007). *The cost of copyright confusion for media literacy.* Washington, DC: Center for Social Media, American University. Retrieved January 2, 2009, from http://www.centerforsocial media.org/resources/publications/the_cost_of_copyright_confusion_for_ media_literacy

Horan, E. (1996). To market: The Dickinson copyright wars. *The Emily Dickinson Journal, 5*(1), 88–120.

Hoskinson, J. (Director). (2009). Episode #05004: Lawrence Lessig [Television series episode]. In S. Colbert & A. Silverman (Executive producers), The Colbert Report. New York, NY: Comedy Central. Retrieved January 8, 2010, from http://colbertnation.com/the-colbert-report-videos/215454/january-08-2009/lawrence-lessig

Hurt, B. (2006). *Beyond beats and rhymes* [DVD]. Northampton, MA: Media Education Foundation.

Jaszi, P. (1991). Toward a theory of copyright: The metamorphosis of "authorship." *Duke Law Journal, 2,* 455–502.

Jaszi, P. (1996). Caught in the net of copyright. Symposium: Innovation and the information environment. *Oregon Law Review, 75,* 299–308.

Joyce, C., Leaffer, M., Jaszi, P., & Ochoa, T. (2003). *Copyright law* (6th ed.). Newark, NJ: Lexis Nexis.

Kennedy, R. (2009, February 10). Artist sues the AP over the Obama image. *New York Times,* p. C1.

Lee, E. (2008). Warming up to user-generated content. *University of Illinois Law Review, 5,* 1459–1548.

Lessig, L. (2004). *Free culture: How big media uses technology and the law to lock down culture and control creativity.* New York: Penguin.

Leval, P. N. (1990). Toward a fair use standard. *Harvard Law Review, 103*(5), 1105–1136.

Levering, M. (1999). What's right about fair-use guidelines for the academic community? *Journal of the American Society for Information Science, 50*(14), 1313–1319.

Livingstone, S. (2004). Media literacy and the challenge of new information and communication technologies. *The Communication Review, 7,* 3–14.

Madison, M. (2006). Fair use and social practices. In P. Yu (Ed.), *Intellectual property and information wealth* (pp. 177–198). Westport, CT: Greenwood.

Madison, M. (2009, January 21). Fairey, Obama and fair use. *Madisonian.net.* Retrieved December 24, 2009, from http://madisonian.net/2009/01/21/fairey-obama-and-fair-use

McLeod, K. & Smith, J. (Producers). (2007). *Freedom of expression: Resistance and repression in the age of intellectual property* [DVD]. Northampton, MA: Media Education Foundation.

Rife, M. (2007). The fair use doctrine: History, application, and implications for (new media) writing teachers. *Computers and Composition 24,* 154–178.

Russell, C. (2004). *Complete copyright: An everyday guide for librarians.* Washington, DC: American Library Association, Office for Information Technology Policy.

Teach Act of 2002, 17 U.S.C. 110. Retrieved January 8, 2010 from http://www.copyright.gov/title17/92chap1.html#110

Triplett, W. (2008, March 3). MPAA canines to dog movie pirates: Malaysian authorities help track counterfeiters. *Variety.* Retrieved December 24,

2009, from http://www.variety.com/article/VR1117981782.html?categoryid=20&cs=1&nid=2562

Tushnet, R. (2004). Copy this essay: How fair use doctrine harms free speech and how copying serves it. *Yale Law Journal, 114*, 535–590.

U.S. Copyright Office. (2007). *Copyright law of the United States.* Title 17 of the U.S. Code. Retrieved December 24, 2009, from http://www.copyright.gov/title17

U.S. Copyright Office. (n.d.). *Reproductions of copyrighted works by educators and librarians.* Circular 21. Retrieved August 27, 2009 from http://www.copyright.gov/circs/circ21.pdf

Valenza, J. (2008, April 1). Fair use and transformativness: It may shake your world. *School Library Journal.* Retrieved December 24, 2009, from http://www.schoollibraryjournal.com/blog/1340000334/post/1420024142.html?q=transformativeness

Von Loehmann, F. (2009, Febuary 3). YouTube's January fair use massacre. *Electronic Frontier Foundation.* Retrieved December 24, 2009, from http://www.eff.org/deeplinks/2009/01/youtubes-january-fair-use-massacre

Warner Bros. Entertainment Inc. and J. K. Rowling v. RDR Books et al., F. Supp.2d 2008 WL 4126736, S.D.N.Y., NO. 07 CIV. 9667 (RPP) (September 8, 2008).

Wilk, J. (2008, February 26). Mybytes teaches a little something about copyright, but what? *Yalsa Blog.* American Library Association. Retrieved December 24, 2009, from http://yalsa.ala.org/blog/2008/02/26/mybytes-teaches-teens-a-little-something-about-copyright-but-what

Index

CORWIN
A SAGE Company

The Corwin logo—a raven striding across an open book—represents the union of courage and learning. Corwin is committed to improving education for all learners by publishing books and other professional development resources for those serving the field of PreK–12 education. By providing practical, hands-on materials, Corwin continues to carry out the promise of its motto: **"Helping Educators Do Their Work Better."**

NCTE National Council of Teachers of English

The National Council of Teachers of English (NCTE) is dedicated to improving the teaching and learning of English and the language arts at all levels of education. Since 1911, NCTE has provided a forum for the profession, an array of opportunities for teachers to continue their professional growth throughout their careers, and a framework for cooperation to deal with issues that affect the teaching of English. For more information, please visit www.ncte.org.